Where Hope Meets You

KATIE T. DUNN

Where Hope Meets You

A DAILY REMINDER OF THE COMFORT AND CONFIDENCE IN GOD'S PROMISES

Published by Iron Hill Press

We would like to thank our storytellers for their vulnerability in sharing their stories with us. It is when we are real with one another about our tragedies, triumphs, and trials, and how the Lord met us in them all, that our lives can be an offering to Him. These storytellers give God all the glory, and we are grateful for their courage to point each of us to the hope found in Jesus.

Published by:

Where Hope Meets You: A Daily Reminder of the Comfort and Confidence in God's Promises

Published by Iron Hill Press and printed in the United States of America.

ironhillpress.com

Library of Congress Cataloging-in-Publication Data is on file with the Library of Congress, Washington, DC.

ISBN: 978-1-970539-06-6

Cover design by Faceout Studio, Brian Mellema

Table of Contents

About These Stories

Throughout the Bible, you see God using the life stories of everyday people to tell about who He is, what His Kingdom is like, and how we should live our short lives here on this earth. Repeatedly, the real-life characters found in Scripture teach us that God is relational, faithful, trustworthy, forgiving, and full of grace. They illustrate God as Redeemer, Provider, Healer, and Savior. They show us His unconditional love for all of humanity, His omnipotent power in impossible situations, and His mysterious purpose in the puzzling moments of life. They give us confidence. They give us assurance. They give us courage. They give us hope.

As you will see in this devotional, God is still working through the power of simple life stories. Each story mentioned in this book is real. Each story was vulnerably shared in front of a live audience. And each story points to the faithfulness of a loving Father. These stories are all part of the *StoryTellers Live* ministry, an organization that consists of communities across the country where everyday women gather in homes to share personal stories of the hope found in Jesus Christ. Those stories are then shared on the weekly *StoryTellers Live* podcast so that this hope may be shared around the world.

At *StoryTellers Live*, we believe that when we take off the masks we all wear daily and share the hard, the ugly, and the difficult—and how the Lord met us in them all—others will discover God in new and profound ways. Our desire is for every person to find God in the details of their own lives and experience a life-giving, thriving relationship with Christ. Through the genuine stories told, our prayer is to increase faith, find freedom in Jesus Christ, and build authentic, transformative community. We believe that is what God can accomplish through the power of story. And we believe the stories in this book will do just that.

For more information on the *StoryTellers Live* ministry, visit our website: www.storytellerslive.org

To listen to each of the stories mentioned in this book in their entirety, go to www.storytellerslive.org/wherehopemeetsyou.

Introduction

The hope found in Jesus is as certain as the rising and setting of the sun each day. Every morning, the light of hope greets you and meets you throughout the day. Every night, the comfort of hope settles your body and brings rest to your soul. This hope is the guaranteed promise of God's presence in your life. It cannot be broken. It cannot be shaken. It cannot be defeated. The hope found in Jesus is the glory of God living in you (Col. 1:27), and it is the very essence of the Christian life.

When I was younger, I always saw hope as a fleeting thought based on the wants and desires of my flesh. My hopes were filled with self-absorbed words and saturated with empty, self-centered wishes. Even when my hopes were attained, the satisfaction that followed was always short-lived and disappointing. My hopes never brought true contentment to the deep longings of my soul. It was only when I met Jesus that I discovered true hope. As I dove into God's Word, I found a hope I never knew existed. A hope based on a person, not a feeling. A hope that was secure, not uncertain. A hope that was expected, not happenstance. A hope that was everlasting, not fleeting. A hope that gave meaning and purpose to my life.

As you will see in the days to come, if you know Jesus, biblical hope is alive and active within you, pointing you toward His promises, directing you toward His presence, turning you toward His peace, and leading you toward His purpose. The hope found in Jesus is a guide and a companion for your present as you navigate the ways of the world, and a compass and a comfort for your future as you set your eyes on eternity. It is the constant assurance from a Father to His child, offered to anyone who will ask (Matt. 7:7-8).

I pray the following daily devotions, and the stories told within them, will open the eyes of your heart to the hope to which God has called you (Eph. 1:18). I pray you would not just know of this hope, but that you would anticipate and experience it (2 Thess. 2:16-17). Most importantly, I pray that you would see how very loved you are by the One who longs to give you this hope (Psalm 130:7). Jesus is real. Jesus is trustworthy. Jesus is faithful. Jesus is hope.

May His hope abound in you.

Day 1

Hope in the Unexpected

"For I know the plans I have for you, declares the LORD, plans for welfare and not for evil, to give you a future and a hope."
—Jeremiah 29:11

Samantha, free-spirited and full of joy, loved her life. She had married her college sweetheart, was raising her firstborn son, enjoyed working at her father's hardware store, and even lived in the house she and her husband had built. In her words, "Everything was rocking along good." And then, "all hell broke loose." Samantha's life changed forever after the birth of her second son and the unexpected statement from her doctor that they were testing her new baby for trisomy 21 (the genetic disorder known as Down Syndrome). Her world stopped. Fear washed over her like a tidal wave. "Wait a minute, what did you say?" Samantha responded to her doctor with surprise and confusion. "Things like this do not happen to people like me. This is not in my plan." Little did Samantha know the joy that lay ahead and the ways God would use His plan, not hers, to turn her fears into faith and bring her to realize that nothing ever happens by accident.

If there is one certainty in this world, it's that life never goes as planned. There are unexpected trials, circumstances, and suffering around every corner. These often leave us disappointed, distraught, and downright disoriented. Relationships end, accidents happen, doors close, jobs are lost, diagnoses are given, and loved ones pass too early. What do you do when the unexpected waves of life hit? Do you topple over? Do you allow the waves to take you under? Perhaps, sometimes, the current of that unexpected wave takes you out to sea, and you might even lose your way to the shore. Child of God, none of these outcomes is what our Father wants for you. God's desire is for you to take that wave head-on, to take a deep breath of His Holy Spirit, dive through the water, and come out on the other side refreshed in your character and renewed in your relationship with Him. But how do you do that? How do you take that tidal wave head-on?

When you focus on the prophet Jeremiah's words in the often-quoted verse of Jeremiah 29:11, you are given hope. God does indeed have a plan for you in the unexpected, and it is for your well-being. However, you must look at the context of this verse to grasp the full meaning of God's promise of a hope-filled future.

When these encouraging words were given to the Israelites, they were in exile in Babylon, longing for God to take them back to their homeland and their old way of life. And, if you just read verse eleven, you'd think "Oh, this sounds good! God's going to solve the situation and solve it quickly!" However, that is not quite what happens. Just a few verses before this verse, God tells the Israelites to get comfortable in this new, unexpected situation. He tells them to "build...settle down...marry...increase in number... and seek...peace and prosperity" (v. 5-7, NIV). This is not what the Israelites wanted to hear! They wanted to be told their suffering was going to end, and they would be going home soon. But God had different plans. Bigger plans. Better plans. God wanted the Israelites to persevere through the trial (which lasted 70 years) and come out stronger and more dependent on Him. This resilience and perseverance were the prosperity and the hope that lay on the other side.

God doesn't always want you to escape from the unexpected. Often, He wants you to learn to thrive in the midst of it. The waves of life give you ample opportunity to strengthen your stance as you plant yourself firmly in your faith, build your confidence as you trust in the Lord's sovereignty and protection, transform your thoughts as you realign them to God's plan for your life, and find rest in knowing God is purposeful in the challenges you face each day. Like the Israelites, cling to the promises found in Jeremiah 29:11, but not in the anticipation of God taking the struggle away from you. Instead, allow the verse to give you a steadfast hope and an eternal perspective as you persevere through the rough waters.

For Samantha, that unexpected day of the birth of her second son led her to new depths in her understanding of God and a new purpose in life. "I have learned so much from this child who is non-verbal," Samantha gratefully and lovingly said. "He knows to just follow what he's taught. And, I was like, I need to take note of this. I just need to do what the will of God is without question. I need to do what Jesus wants me to do. And, then, I thought, you know, I've never talked about this kind of stuff." What Jesus was calling Samantha (and three other mothers who had children with disabilities) to do was to start the East Alabama Exceptional Foundation. This nonprofit organization serves people with intellectual and developmental disabilities and provides opportunities for them.

As she reflects on her journey, Samantha now understands God's love in new and profound ways. "The worst thing that has happened to me has turned my life into something that would have never been," she said joyfully. "Nothing happens by accident. No thread of experience, good or bad, is wasted. When it appears to be that way, we just have to remind ourselves that we are simply looking at the backside of a tapestry. And the One weaving it together knows precisely what He's doing."

A Closing Prayer

Lord, thank you for the hope you give me in the unexpected waves of life as they draw me closer to you for stamina and strength. I praise you for being a trustworthy Father who helps me navigate the waters. Remind me that you alone "rule the raging sea; (and) when its waves surge, you still them" (Psalm 89:9 CSB). Equip me to stand firmly in my faith and to pass peacefully through the waters with the indwelling of Your Holy Spirit. Amen.

To listen to Samantha's story, go to www.storytellerslive.org/wherehopemeetsyou and look for "Hope in the Unexpected."

Day 2

Hope in Suffering

"Not only that, but we rejoice in our sufferings, knowing that suffering produces endurance, and endurance produces character, and character produces hope, and hope does not put us to shame, because God's love has been poured into our hearts through the Holy Spirit who has been given to us."
—Romans 5:3–5

Ginger was in seventh grade when she saw her mother and father accept Jesus Christ as their Lord and Savior. "I saw Christ become the center of a home that wasn't the center before," Ginger said. "It really took notice in my life." As Ginger continued through adolescence and early adulthood, she witnessed her parents develop a deep love for God's Word and a heart for those who didn't know Jesus. She said her father lived by the mantra, "Only two things last forever: the Word of God and the souls of men and women. If you're not investing in those two things, you're wasting your time." It was a foundational truth that was instrumental in Ginger's life, but one she never fully grasped until the year that extreme devastation hit her family.

Ginger's father suddenly passed away, leaving a terrible void in her family's heart. And then, six short months later, the unimaginable happened. Ginger's 17-year-old daughter was killed in a terrible car accident. "We were just in shock. I knew in my heart that to be absent from the body, you are present with the Lord. But this sickness just came over me." As Ginger left her daughter in the hospital, she was overwhelmed with the reality of her grief. "I'll never forget just sitting there in the car. It was silent on the way home. And, all of a sudden, I thought, I've got to talk to the Lord. I said, 'Lord, I know you said to give thanks in all things. Please bring them on. Please bring to mind one thing, just one thing I can be thankful for.'"

How do you give thanks to God during intense suffering and sorrow? How do you look towards the heavens when your earthly world is spinning out of control? How do you, as the Apostle Paul encourages you to do in Romans 5:3, "glory in your sufferings"? Ask anyone who has buried a loved one or endured the pain of disease or experienced unfairness and injustice or lost relationships and jobs, and many will tell you that their natural inclination in the face of adversity isn't to praise the Lord. Instead, it's to question Him, lose faith in Him, sit in anger against Him, get immersed in bitterness towards Him, and allow grief to guide you instead of Him.

As much as we don't like to hear it, the crux of the Christian life rests in trusting that the Holy Spirit is doing some of His best work during the hardest and most trying times of our lives. You read Romans 5:3-5, and you think, "glory in my sufferings"? There's no way I can exalt the name of the Lord in this. I can't praise His name when all I want to do is shout out in rage. I can't lift my eyes to eternity when my head is being pulled down to despair. I can't direct my soul to sing when my heart is in pain. And the truth is that you can't, at least not on your own. This is where the "unseen" work of the Holy Spirit takes place.

When Paul wrote these words to those living in Rome, he knew firsthand what a life of suffering looked like. In fact, he probably knew this truth better than anyone. He had endured multiple beatings, imprisonments, hunger, and constant danger from various people and situations. But he also knew the development of his character and the extreme hope he had in Jesus Christ were a direct result of his perseverance through the intense tribulations he had endured. He knew the Lord was with him in the suffering, working all things for good (Rom. 8:28), and he knew without a doubt that suffering and glory were connected. Paul goes into detail about this concept in his second letter to the Corinthians, saying, "for our light and momentary troubles are achieving for us an eternal glory that far outweighs them all" (2 Cor. 4:17, NIV).

God is working in the unseen moments of your life. Those moments when you are crying out to Him to answer your prayers. Those moments when you are questioning His ways, wondering what He is doing. Those moments when all you can do is fall on your face before Him and beg for His presence to be felt. God does indeed have a good and glorious purpose in allowing the pain you are experiencing. Does it make it easier? Not necessarily. But finding purpose in the pain does make it tolerable in the temporary. So, today, let yourself be motivated by the glory of God by immersing yourself in the truths of His Word and the love He longs to pour into your heart through the power of His Holy Spirit.

Ginger struggled for a long time to know how to exalt the Lord amid her heartbreak. It wasn't until the Holy Spirit revealed the love God had for her, and she contemplated the pain He experienced on the day of Jesus' crucifixion. "Willingly, God chose for His Son to die," Ginger explained. "It just overwhelmed me that He would choose to go through the pain I was experiencing." As Ginger contemplated the sacrifice of Jesus, the Lord continued to work in her heart as He revealed to her these words: "God is still working in the unseen. I think about the disciples and the cross. Can you imagine how devastated they were? They were so distraught. And they thought, "What is God doing? And yet that was the greatest act of love and the greatest sacrifice. And so, when I can't see what I want to see - I can't see my daughter - I remember that God is faithful in the unseen, and He's going to do great things. The struggle has produced things that will last forever, things that will change me forever. The only things that last forever sometimes are the unseen."

A Closing Prayer

Lord, I know you love me, and you can turn every trial I walk through into an opportunity for good in my life. Help me to feel your presence in the unseen, especially in those moments where I feel as if I've been forgotten. Father, focus my eyes on you and your glory in the midst of my suffering and give me faith to not lose hope. Amen.

To listen to Ginger's story, go to www.storytellerslive.org/wherehopemeetsyou and look for "Hope in Suffering."

Day 3

Hope in Persistent Prayers

"Rejoice in hope, be patient in tribulation,
be constant in prayer."
—Romans 12:12

When Gail was 17, she met Jim. He was tall and handsome, and he swept her off her feet. A short 112 days later, she married him. And two weeks shy of her 18th birthday, she gave birth to their first daughter. It was a whirlwind romance that appeared nearly perfect until Gail saw Jim slowly changing before her eyes. "When he was good, he was good; he wanted the best for us. But when he was angry, he was not good," Gail recalled. "It was like my dreams were shattered. It wasn't a 'happy ever after.' It was like I met someone I didn't know. It was almost like the devil moved in." Jim's anger continued to escalate over the years, and while he never physically abused Ginger, his words would cut deeply.

Gail was living a life paralyzed by fear. "I lived a life of knowing I never knew what was going to upset him and cause him to be mad." A devout follower of Jesus, Gail was determined not to leave. So, she began pouring herself into God and His Word. "The

Lord was just stirring in my heart through all of this. I just started crying out to the Lord. And He heard my cry." As Ginger pursued the Lord, He continued to draw her closer to Him and gave her the strength not only to survive in her marriage but also to thrive in her life and in her walk with Him. "I knew God was directing me, and the Word became alive to me. It was at that time that God put me in a little prayer group, and I learned how to pray. I went through every room of my house with my Bible open, reading Scripture. Every spot in my house, I just claimed for Jesus. It was spiritual warfare."

Oftentimes, amid the impossible circumstances of life, the thought of being still and going to God in prayer seems like the most passive action you can take. Your unrelenting flesh screams, "*Do something*!" to correct the situation. Read a self-help book, talk to someone for advice, check out of the relationship, leave the job, or ignore the problem altogether; all of these are just ways to change the circumstances and relieve yourself of the pain. However, it's in these moments that God waits patiently for you to come to Him.

God knows your "struggle is not against flesh and blood...but against the powers of this dark world" (Eph. 6:12), and He knows the only way to win the battles you will face is to include Him in the fight. He even gives you specific armor to wear to prepare for battle: the belt of truth, the breastplate of righteousness, feet sandaled with the gospel of peace, the shield of faith, the helmet of salvation, and the sword of the Spirit, which is the Word of God. Then, you are told to pray at all times with every prayer and request (Eph. 6:14-18). The idea is, after you put on the armor, your action step is to pray, and this act is the single most important and powerful spiritual practice of the Christian faith.

The Bible is full of supernatural responses to prayer as people persistently prayed for themselves and others. Moses prayed and changed the course of history (Exodus 32:11-14). Hannah prayed, and a prophet was born (1 Samuel 1:10-20). Peter prayed, and the church was established (Acts 4:24-31). Jesus prayed, and all humanity was redeemed (Luke 22:42). There is no doubt that prayer draws each of us closer to God as we rest in His sovereignty and trustworthiness.

The Apostle Paul knew firsthand the power of prayer as he repeatedly prayed for fruitfulness in God's Kingdom. The result was the spreading of the gospel message of Christ. In Romans 12, Paul caps off his brief series of Christ-like instructions with persistent prayer as the key to the hope-filled Christian life. The word "persistent" in the original Greek conveys the idea that you remain and endure as you bravely and calmly face your situation. You persevere under your misfortunes and your trials, and you hold fast to your faith in Christ. This tells us prayer isn't always easy. It can be hard work. It requires strength, endurance, patience, and courage. But rest assured, it will change your life and the lives of others.

So, be encouraged. Your Father in Heaven hears your desperate cries and pleas. And He's working even if you can't see it. Even if you can't feel it, He's working. Continue to pour your heart out to Him. Wear your armor every day. Hold fast to your faith. Be persistent in your prayers, and watch God move.

The Lord did a mighty work in Gail while she persevered in her tumultuous marriage through the power of prayer. As she leaned into the Lord, He worked deeply in her heart to love her husband through the overflow of His love for her. As Jim got older, he was diagnosed with cancer, and Gail desperately wanted him to know Jesus and accept Him as his Savior. So, she continued in her prayers. Slowly, God began to turn Jim's heart, and he began to ask questions about Jesus and Heaven. Before he passed away, Jim accepted Christ as his Savior and made things right with his family. Gail sweetly said, "That was the faithfulness of prayer for someone. My word to you in all of this is: don't give up praying. You might be married to an impossible person; it might be your mom, your dad, or your kids. Don't quit praying because God hears those prayers. Be faithful in your prayer, keep praying, and watch God move."

A Closing Prayer

Lord, thank you for the gift of a relationship with you through prayer and for the hope found in and through my prayer life. Thank you for listening intently when I speak. I ask you to give me the strength and endurance to remain persistent in my prayers as I wait patiently for you to move. Father, I trust you above all else. May your will be done. Amen.

To listen to Gail's story, go to www.storytellerslive.org/wherehopemeetsyou and look for "Hope in Persistent Prayers."

Day 4

Hope in Rest

"Come to me, all who labor and are heavy laden,
and I will give you rest."
—Matthew 11:28

Courtney was great at running on the "treadmill of life," constantly doing and performing for others. "I was the entertainer, the organizer, the connector, the leader; I could entertain a crowd, and I liked the attention." As she attended college, her striving, achieving, and working became a way of life. She liked the feeling of succeeding, and she soon bought into the lie that she was only loved if she was doing. "It wasn't a lie my parents told me and not something any coach or anyone told me, but somehow I got the message, I'm only loved if I'm doing something or I'm productive; that's when God loves me, or that's when others love me." This was a lie Courtney believed for years.

As she got older, she found herself hopping on and off the treadmill, running from one activity to the next, looking for her worth in the things of this world rather than in Christ. Until, one day, the Holy Spirit tugged at Courtney's heart. She began to think about her motives, and her eyes were opened. "I wasn't doing it for the Lord, I was doing it for me," Courtney stated matter-of-factly. "I would leave every achievement feeling empty and unfulfilled."

Courtney started leaning into the Lord and asking Him how to live her life. "What would it look like if I involved you in these decisions? What if I decided what I was going to do was going to be based on discernment, based on what the Holy Spirit was telling me to do, what He wanted me to do with my life?" These were questions that shifted Courtney's life as the Lord began nudging her to find her identity in Him alone. It was a nudging that led her to a three-year sabbatical of rest.

"Jesus, Take the Wheel" was singer Carrie Underwood's first number-one hit. The song's underlying message is to exchange our insatiable need for control for peace from the one who controls it all. It's an age-old choice that generations of Believers have struggled with. After all, a spirit of surrender, an attitude of humility, and a posture of rest don't come naturally. We think that if we plan more, do more, and achieve more, then we'll be accepted, loved, and content. But, as is often the case, the ways of the world are contrary to the ways of God.

God's desire is for us to live utterly and completely dependent on Him. He longs for us to take off the heavy and burdensome yoke of the world and put on His light and easy yoke, allowing Him to lead and direct our days (Matthew 11:28-30). Yet, we continue to buy into the lie that the ways of the world are better. And much like the Old Testament Israelites in the wilderness, we "stiff-neck" the Lord.

In Exodus 33, we read that the Israelites had stubbornly resisted God and relied on their old ways of worship, and God's anger burned against them because of it. Twice, He called them "a stiff-necked people." The image depicts an ox resisting the farmer's guidance by stiffening its neck. The farmer knows the best way to plow the field, but the animal refuses to surrender and follow. Fortunately, the Israelites desperately wanted to make things right with the Lord, so they humbled themselves before Him, laying their ornaments at the base of Mount Horeb as a symbol of their surrendered hearts (and necks).

We then see Moses boldly praying on behalf of the Israelites for the Lord's presence. He was determined to have God as close to Israel as possible before the daunting task of taking over the Promised Land. After his request, the Lord faithfully replied, "My Presence will go with you, and I will give you rest" (v.14). Keep in mind, this was not a physical rest. After all, they were about to go into battle. Instead, it was a spiritual rest, a rest from chaos, confusion, worry, stress, and from the effort to control everything. It was a move away from these things and into a rest of reliance, courage, confidence, and trust in the Lord. Today, God invites each of us into that same rest. Hebrews 4:1 tells us, "Therefore, while the promise of entering his rest still stands, let us fear lest any of you should seem to have failed to reach it."

The word "rest" in this verse depicts the beautiful illustration of the calming of the winds. There is a peacefulness and a stillness that surrounds it because you trust in the one who directs it all. Just like the Israelites who were facing imminent battles ahead in the Promised Land, we place our complete trust in the Lord as we walk through each day of our lives. We enter His rest by faith as we stop relying on our own efforts and become solely dependent on God, yielding completely to the promises of His Word and immersing our thoughts in the grace of our salvation.

Today, enter God's rest by setting aside intentional time with the Lord each day. Practice spiritual stillness. Cease striving. Seek solace in His presence. Activate your faith and experience the Holy Spirit calming the winds of your world.

Courtney found that her rest in the Lord resulted in an internal interruption in her system. In her words, "I'm a different person. I am healed from the inside. I feel more peace and less rattled." She also discovered the truth that God didn't love her for what she did for Him. He loved her for who she was. "I've learned deeply in my soul that God really loves me. I've learned that true margin, true resting, is a powerful healing agent. I can be used for His glory in astounding ways if I'll only pause, rest in Him, and trust He knows the very best plan for my life."

A Closing Prayer

Father, I praise you for the promise of rest found in your presence and the gift of calmness that comes from complete trust in you. Help me to surrender to your light and easy yoke as I let go of the lies of the world and look to you to control my life. Take the wheel of my life and guide my every step and direct my every decision. Allow my life to be a light to those around me who are looking for your peace. Amen.

To listen to Courtney's story, go to www.storytellerslive.org/wherehopemeetsyou and look for "Hope in Rest."

Day 5

Hope in Parenting

"But this I call to mind, and therefore I have hope:
The steadfast love of the LORD never ceases;
his mercies never come to an end;
they are new every morning;
great is your faithfulness."
—Lamentations 3:21–23

Being an overprotective mother was Ruth's gift. Her fears of her children's future, coupled with an abundance of anxiety, created a posture of striving to be the best mom she could be. "The facade of control was there," Ruth recalled. However, "When they got older, I could not control everything. It just sent me into a tailspin of constant worry. I knew the most important thing in their lives was to know Jesus. But trusting God with their lives was very hard."

Like most parents, Ruth wanted to protect her children from any heartache, but it was the little hurts and disappointments that began to shatter her soul. "It was the rejection that was making me so upset; that my child I love so much was getting rejected." Soon, Ruth began spiraling in her thoughts, questioning every life choice she had made as a mother. Until one day, the Lord opened her eyes to the pain she was experiencing. "I thought about all this rejection. Then, I thought, Jesus was rejected in a big way. Our kids are going to be rejected. We are going to be rejected. I was not trusting the Lord."

Parenting is not for the faint of heart. It is filled with a plethora of emotions. Deep unrelenting love and overwhelming joy mixed with quiet heartbreak and anxiety-driven fear; this is the incredible gift of guardianship. It is one of the few roles in life where your emotions can take you on a roller coaster ride, leaving you on top of the world one minute and defeated the next. And if you aren't contemplative of your own self-motives and intentional in your prayers and your trust in God, it's a place where you can easily begin to find your identity, self-worth, and purpose. And, when that happens, the enemy has gotten a foothold on you, and consequently, your child. But there is hope!

First, every parent must recognize their child is a gift from the Lord (Psalm 127:3). He knew them before they were born (Jer. 1:5). He alone is their Creator, Sustainer, and Savior (Col. 1:16-17). They belong to Him (Eze. 18:4). These truths should empower you as well as release you from the heavy burden that the outcome of your child's life solely depends on your role as the perfect parent. There is no perfect parent. God calls you to demonstrate (to the best of your ability) a life that reflects Him, to speak with love and wisdom that honors His ways, and to live by His Word and point your children to it. He wants you to be the best possible steward of the gift He has given you. However, He also knows you are a flawed sinner. And so, He comes alongside you, giving you inner strength and guidance, transforming your heart to become more like His along the way.

Second, God's grace follows you as His mercies are new every morning (Lam. 3:23). And, wow, do we need those mercies as parents! No matter how bad the past day was, how awful the circumstances are, or how hurtful the situation is, God provides a constant supply of compassion, and because of that, you can face the challenges of parenting with faith and hope. You rest knowing that what others might mean for evil, God can use for good (Gen. 50:20), and you are freed from the fear of not being the perfect parent and released from the pressure to protect your child and ensure their success.

Third, and most importantly, while you acknowledge "parent" as your earthly title for your child, embracing "prayer warrior" as your spiritual title is essential to tapping into the Holy Spirit's power as you navigate the waters of parenthood. Often, as mothers and fathers, we think of praying over our children as passive, and as a result, it becomes our last resort. We think we need to do something for our child or say something to them to place them on a trajectory we believe is pertinent to their emotional, mental, physical, and spiritual health. The greatest action you can take, the greatest words you can speak, the greatest eternal impact you can make are prayers offered up on your child's behalf. Don't let the enemy deceive you into thinking praying is useless. If you aren't praying over your child each day, begin doing so now!

So, whether your child is in the elementary years and you need physical strength, or in the adolescent years and you need emotional strength, or in adulthood and you need mental strength, find peace, comfort, and hope knowing that God is with you. He is for you. He will lead you and strengthen you with the Holy Spirit as your guide. Your child is His. He is working on their behalf. He has a purpose for their life. And He loves them more than you do.

For Ruth, the Lord used a health crisis in her family to propel her on the journey of trusting Him with her children. After the near-death of her father, she said, "My perspective completely changed. I thought, if He can sustain me through that trauma, I can bring my broken little things that I'm worried about to Him." As Ruth brought the broken pieces in her heart regarding her children before the Lord, she began seeing life as a mom through a new lens and a new purpose. "What we want to strive for with our kids is not how popular they are, how good they are at this or that, but instead instilling compassion for other people and love for all people. Jesus is the one who can and will change your life, just like He has changed mine."

A Closing Prayer

Lord, thank you for the gift of parenting and guardianship, and for the hope I have that you alone will guide me. Thank you for entrusting me to lead the next generation towards you. When I fail in this endeavor, cover me with your mercies and lead me to your truth. Help me to find my identity, self-worth, and purpose in you alone, and to parent from the foundation of my faith. I commit my child into your hands and trust you with their life. Amen.

To listen to Ruth's story, go to www.storytellerslive.org/wherehopemeetsyou and look for "Hope in Parenting."

Day 6

Hope in Anxiety

"Humble yourselves, therefore, under the mighty hand of God
so that at the proper time he may exalt you,
casting all your anxieties on him,
because he cares for you."
—1 Peter 5:6–7

Brittany grew up in a wonderful home environment, filled with great memories and loving parents. As a pastor's kid, she was raised in the church and took part in all the ministry opportunities. *Mission Friends* and *Girls in Action*, as well as mission trips and Bible drills, were part of Brittany's teenage years. "I was the poster child for the 90s Christian kid," she laughed, "I don't think I had a secular CD until I was in high school. I was probably a little sheltered." However, out of nowhere, in the midst of this nurturing, faith-filled environment, Brittany found herself beginning to feel physical, mental, and emotional symptoms she couldn't control. "I can remember sitting in high school with my throat closing in, hands sweating, and the feeling of needing to escape the room. And it would happen in church, too." As Brittany opened up to her parents about what was happening in her body, she soon discovered anxiety, panic attacks, and depression spanned her mother's side of the family. It was a revelation that began her journey of learning that sometimes the Lord allows struggles in your life so you will recognize your need for Him.

We all know anxiety shows no favoritism. It can rear its ugly head abruptly, affecting anyone, regardless of age, occupation, or spiritual maturity. It is simply a symptom of the human condition. And as we see in Jesus' agony in the garden of Gethsemane, it is not always the result of a crisis of faith.

The night before His crucifixion on the cross, Jesus, fully God, but also fully man, experienced feelings that today we might associate with anxiety. Is the word "anxious" the best way to describe Jesus? Maybe not, but there is no doubt that He was deeply emotionally troubled. The scope of the trial He was about to undertake washed over Him as He cried out, "My soul is very sorrowful, even to death." (Matthew 26:38). And, as He prayed more earnestly, we even see that His sweat fell like drops of blood falling to the ground (Luke 22:44). If ever there was a scene in the Bible of someone enduring physical, emotional, mental, and spiritual turmoil all at once, it is the picture of our Savior the day of His looming death.

However, Jesus also gives us hope for this impending day. While His flesh lamented the suffering to come on the cross, we see His Spirit hyper-focused on completing God's will for His life. He knew that while His fear and anxiety were real, His Father in Heaven was sovereign over it all. Jesus trusted the Father, knowing He would use the trial of the cross to accomplish good for all Creation. It was Jesus' humility in this divine moment of human distress that delivered the gift of eternal life given to you and me today.

Humility, mixed with a deep faith that God is sovereign over it all, can move you to become more like Christ in times of anxiety and fear, growing you in your dependence on the Lord and helping you relinquish your will to His will for your life. In 1 Peter 5:6-7, Peter reminds us of the importance of humility and faith in moments of anxiousness as he says, "Humble yourselves, therefore, under the mighty hand of God so that at the proper time he may exalt you, casting all your anxieties on him, because he cares for you."

Two action steps are given to us here: First, humble your anxious thoughts to God's throne and submit to His plan for your life. God may guide you to prayer, to Christian counseling, to doctors and/or medicine (or to all three as He did for Brittany), but you must first humble yourself before Him and relinquish your control over the situation. Second, you are told to cast onto God (throw away from you) the pressures, burdens, and worries of your life. This step requires effort, self-reflection, concentration, and most importantly, faith. You must believe that the Lord genuinely cares for you. And as a result, you cast your difficulties on Him, knowing He will lead you to His best for your life.

Anxiety is real. Fears exist. Worries are certain. And there is no simple, easy solution. Our role as followers of Jesus is to trust in the one who is over all, and through all, and in all (Eph. 4:6) God is supreme, God is sustaining, and God is indwelling in you. Persist in pouring yourself out to Him as a drink offering (Phil. 2:17) and rejoice knowing He can and will use your struggles to bring glory to Him and purpose to you.

God eventually led Brittany to a "three-prong approach" to her anxiety and panic attacks. She credits God's grace, Christian therapy, and modern medicine for saving her life. She began cognitive behavior therapy and was able to understand more clearly the reasons behind her emotional and mental struggles. And, while she still suffers at times, she's learned to be at peace with it. "Paul, in Scripture, talks about the thorn in his flesh. Even though I've gotten to a good place, it is still a part of my life. I refuse to let Satan get a hold of where my mind can go. I've learned how to navigate those attacks better." And as Brittany has learned to allow the Lord to be strong where she was weak, her humility and her faith in submitting to His will have become a way of life for her.

Brittany knows not to let tomorrow's worries steal the energy God has given her for today. "Scripture is clear that Jesus has given us exactly what we need for today," Brittany said, "I love using the Lord's prayer as an outline for my prayer life. God, give me what I need for today. Give me my daily bread. God gives me what I need for today, and then, tomorrow, His mercies are new. He sees me. He loves me. He cares and knows when I'm in a bad place. All we can do is just take everything one day at a time."

A Closing Prayer

Lord, thank you for calling me to cast my anxiety on you. Thank you for being a Father who cares for me and my anxious thoughts and for being a Son who knows firsthand what it's like to feel debilitated by them. Help me to have hope and see you in moments of suffering and help me to turn my anxiousness into glory for you. I praise you for being sovereign over it all as I approach my life as a drink offering to you. Amen.

To listen to Brittany's story, go to www.storytellerslive.org/wherehopemeetsyou and look for "Hope in Anxiety."

Day 7

Hope in Surrender

"But he said to me, 'My grace is sufficient for you,
for my power is made perfect in weakness.' Therefore
I will boast all the more gladly of my weaknesses,
so that the power of Christ may rest upon me."
—2 Corinthians 12:9

At a young age, Erica acknowledged Jesus Christ as her Lord and Savior. She wanted Him to save her from her sins, and she wanted to go to Heaven. But as she got older, she also realized she wanted to retain control of her own life. "I didn't want to submit to God's rule and reign over my life. I thought I could orchestrate my life better than my Heavenly Father, who made me."

As Erica entered her junior year of high school, this deep-seated desire for control suddenly took an unhealthy turn. Before she knew it, she found herself on the subtle yet slippery slope of an eating disorder. "I developed an unhealthy relationship with exercise, and then started restricting what I ate," Erica reflected. "I became fearful of gaining weight and became obsessed with my appearance. My worth became attached to the number on the scale and the size of my clothes. And, on top of that, I liked the feeling of being in control of my food, my weight, my body, and people's perception of me."

Erica's desire for control and need for others' approval only intensified as she started college, leading her to a crossroads in her faith. "My eating disorder revealed my pride, my desire for control, and my rebellion against God and His ways. I needed Jesus to treat my disordered heart and realign my priorities." Erica became desperately dependent on God as she realized she couldn't fight this battle alone. It was this posture that led her to surrender to His sovereignty and His healing hands of grace. "I saw my sin and my mess, and I also saw my deep need for a Savior as I had never seen before. And I wanted to trust Jesus, and I needed to trust Jesus. I wanted to follow Him."

The word "surrender" carries a connotation of loss. Loss of victory and power. Loss of control and freedom. Loss of dignity and respect. Embracing the idea of surrendering feels unnatural, to say the least. It feels illogical and uncertain. It feels passive and weak. It feels like defeat and failure, a "waving of the white flag," so to speak. Yet, in the spiritual realm, mastering the art of surrendering and giving thanks in your weaknesses is one of the most victorious and powerful actions you can take in your life.

Repeatedly in Scripture, the Lord's plans are revealed to those who deny their flesh and surrender to God. Abraham surrendered his life to God and became the father of many nations (Gen. 17:4-5). Hannah surrendered her son, Samuel, and a mighty prophet and leader was given to Israel (1 Samuel 1:27-28). Mary and Joseph surrendered their reputations and respect, and the Savior of the world was born (Matthew 1:18-25). The Apostle Paul surrendered his prestigious position among the Pharisees, and the Christian church was established (Acts 9:1-31). It's pretty clear that the process of surrendering is tied to eternal purposes here on earth.

But surrendering doesn't come naturally. Giving up control of your life and yielding your whole self (your emotions, your gifts, your struggles) to the Lord is a continuous choice that requires humility, especially in seasons where taking control seems like the only way to alleviate the pain. In his second letter to the Corinthians, Paul reveals the secret God gave him in making surrendering less painful: "My grace is sufficient for you, for my power is made perfect in weakness" (2 Cor. 12:9). This simple yet divine statement led Paul to not just surrender to the Lord but to boast and delight in his weaknesses, insults, hardships, persecutions, and difficulties. He recognized surrender and weakness were actually his strengths (v.10). God's answer to surrender was to focus on His grace, and it's His answer to you today.

So, focus on the unconditional love that encompasses God's grace. Lay down your "go to" weapons of war and allow the Lord to take control. Believe God has a plan for your life, and His plan is good. And rest assured knowing your Father in Heaven is a wise and compassionate conqueror. He overcomes you to bless you. Greater surrender brings deeper intimacy, greater surrender fills you with the Holy Spirit, and greater surrender makes you more like Christ.

Recognizing that God's power is made perfect in her weakness was a huge turning point for Erica. And as a result, she began practicing what she refers to as "palms up," a method in which, in moments of distress or when she feels the need to be in control, she physically clenches her fists and then releases them, palms up, signifying that she is handing them over to the Lord. "It is such a powerful picture of surrendering control to Christ and trusting Him with our lives," Erica said. "When we let go and trust God with our lives and our circumstances, not only are we communicating our trust in Him, but we are also better able to receive by faith the gifts He has for us. And this is such a posture of surrender. And it's not just a surrender of some things; these things are mine to control, and then you can have the rest. It's a whole surrender. It acknowledges God's sovereignty and authority over my life. It expresses my trust that God will take care of me. It acknowledges that everything that I have belongs to the Lord. God has made a path. We just need to open our hands, be expectant of what God has for us, and take the step forward in obedience."

A Closing Prayer

Father, I thank you for your good and perfect plan for my life, and for calling me to surrender to it. I praise you for taking my weaknesses and turning them into strengths that you can use for my good and your glory. Help me, Lord, to trust you more and relinquish control to your purposes. I lay down my will and embrace yours. Amen.

To listen to Erica's story, go to www.storytellerslive.org/wherehopemeetsyou and look for "Hope in Surrender."

Day 8

Hope in Healing

"Trust in the LORD with all your heart, and do not lean on your own understanding. In all your ways acknowledge him, and he will make straight your paths."
—Proverbs 3:5–6

Juleigh was 28 years old and newly married with a six-week-old baby girl when she heard the news that shook her world. "You've got a tumor in your eye, and I'm pretty sure it's cancer," her doctor said. In the weeks to come, Juleigh found out she had ocular melanoma, a rare type of eye cancer. Her mind flooded with questions, especially about her future. That is, until the Lord led her to the familiar verse of Jeremiah 29:11. "I kept saying it over and over," Juleigh said, "Lord, you're telling me you've got good plans for me, plans for me to prosper and not to harm me and to give me hope and a future. And that's all I want right now: a future. I was surrendering. And, I remember then just having this peace." Ultimately, Juleigh had to have surgery to remove her eye, but as she recited that verse, her fears were alleviated. "I felt so much like God was holding me and carrying me through like I had never felt before." With huge praises, Juleigh's surgery was successful, and while she had to learn to navigate life with one eye, she went on with a thankful heart.

Then, 14 years later, the unimaginable happened. Juleigh had been experiencing intense pain in her abdomen that radiated up to her back. She was diagnosed with pancreatic cancer. Again, those familiar shock waves hit, and disbelief settled in. Juleigh knew she needed to go to God's Word, and the Lord sweetly led her to Proverbs 3:5-6. It was a turning point where Juleigh said she felt God's familiar peace again, "He's got me in His hands, and all He wants is for me to depend completely on Him."

"I am the Lord, who heals you" (Ex. 15:26). This was God's declaration to the Israelites after they made their escape from slavery in Egypt and walked through the Red Sea on dry ground. This Hebrew name, "Jehovah Rapha," was a promise given to the people as they trusted and obeyed God, who led them to the Promised Land. Trust and obey, and you will be healed. What does this mean for you and me today? Is this a physical healing, a spiritual healing, or both? In God's infinite wisdom and higher ways, the answer is a resounding "yes" to both.

The hope Jehovah Rapha desires for each of us comes from trusting His character, sovereignty, and promises in His Word while seeking His strength, comfort, and peace in prayer. It is the hope that strengthens and steadies you as you seek miraculous healing in the insurmountable challenges of life. And, yes, God still performs miracles. Throughout the New Testament, we see Jesus demonstrating His healing power over demons, illnesses, diseases, and countless other ways, including death. God is a miraculous healer by nature. Healing is a part of who He is.

If you or someone you know is suffering from an ailment (whether physical, mental, emotional, or spiritual), don't think for a second that God cannot heal the situation and use the suffering for good. It's in these moments that the enemy wants to steal your joy and cause you to doubt the love and goodness of your Father, a Father whose desire is for you to be healthy in every way. The truth is, God sent His Son, Jesus, to die for you because He wants you to be well. Sometimes, that results in physical healing here on this earth. Other times, there are layers to His healing that can only take place in eternity with God, promised to all who believe.

So, like the story of the desperate father pleading for the miraculous healing of his son, we cry out to the Lord, "I believe; help my unbelief!" (Mark 9:24). In the interim, we trust He alone is the Great Physician. We trust His healing hands are infinitely greater than our own. We trust He hears our prayers and will increase our faith. We trust He will give us a hope and a future, making our paths straight.

Juleigh's course of treatment for her pancreatic cancer wasn't easy. Her tumor was close to a major artery, causing her to undergo eight months of potent chemotherapy to try to shrink it. Through the prayers of many, Juleigh kept her eyes focused on God as she repeated, "I will trust you. This is not my understanding. Lord, your plan is bigger and better than mine." As the chemo did its work, Juleigh was finally ready for surgery. It took 5 ½ hours as her doctor removed part of her pancreas, part of her colon, part of her stomach, a kidney, an adrenal gland, and her spleen. The follow-up plan was for her to undergo chemotherapy again after the surgery to kill any loose cells. However, in God's miraculous healing hands, her pathology report came back with not one viable cell found. "In all my years of doing this," the doctor told Juleigh's husband, "this has never happened. There is no need to do chemotherapy because there's nothing there. It's all dead. Your wife was right when she said there was Somebody bigger using my hands, because that surgery is a true miracle."

Juleigh recognizes that not everyone's story ends like hers. She doesn't understand the reasons why, but she does know God saved her to call her to share her story. "Sometimes we think things are way too big to ask God. We think He can't work that miracle because it's not a medical possibility, that doesn't happen, or this is way too broken. Whether it's a relationship or a disease or a child that's gone away or whatever it is, we feel like i''s a lost cause. I'm here to tell you that He really is a big God, and He wants us to pray, and pray believing big."

A Closing Prayer

Lord, thank you for being the Great Physician, my Jehovah Rapha. I acknowledge every ailment, illness, and disease bows down to your name. Father, increase my belief in your omnipotence and help me to trust in your love and sovereignty, especially in moments where I am desperate for your healing power. Thank you for the hope you have given me that one day there will be no more death, sorrow, crying, or pain. What a glorious day that will be! Amen.

To listen to Juleigh's story, go to www.storytellerslive.org/wherehopemeetsyou and look for "Hope in Healing."

Day 9

Hope in the Providence of God

"Many are the plans in the mind of a man,
but it is the purpose of the LORD that will stand."
—Proverbs 19:21

"This is a story of love lost, and love found again and the providence of God," Laurel stated. It started the summer when she met Adam at youth camp. It was a friendship that turned into a relationship, which five years later turned into marriage. Soon after, they had children, and "life was good," Laurel said. Then, one morning, Adam wasn't feeling well. After many doctor visits, it was determined he needed what was called "a routine sinus surgery." However, on the day of his surgery, doctors discovered his problems weren't stemming from just his sinuses. Adam had cancer. The months that followed carried with them multiple rounds of chemotherapy, radiation, and a difficult surgery. But, to their dismay, a few months later, the cancer came back. And in three short weeks, Adam passed away. "I was a widow at 36. Adam was only 33, and I had three babies," Laurel recalled. "I do not know how people go through things like this without God by their side. My sister told me, 'We will never understand the why on this side of heaven,' and we won't. It's my story. And all I had was hope and faith."

Some people call the ways of the world "destiny" or "fate." Some call it chance or coincidence. Some call it luck of the draw. But, for the Christian, the events of our lives are all the providence of God. God is lovingly in complete control of *all* things, and through His providence, He accomplishes His will. Rest assured, God is not a passive observer of the world we live in or the life you lead. Time and again in Scripture, we see God's invisible hands working behind the scenes, taking what Satan meant for evil and destruction and turning it into goodness and purpose.

In the Book of Genesis, you have the story of Joseph: cruelly sold into slavery by his brothers, subsequently put into prison through deception, and ultimately given the gift of interpretation that led to his being promoted to second in command to Pharaoh in Egypt. Even Joseph himself was able to see God's providential hand in his life as he forgave his brothers and said, "As for you, you meant evil against me, but God meant it for good, to bring it about that many people should be kept alive, as they are today" (Gen. 50:20).

The Book of Ruth is the story of a series of seemingly chance events. With themes of tragedy, integrity, and generosity, you see God at work through a declaration of devotion to a widowed mother-in-law, the happenstance of gleaning in a field of favor, and the unforeseen marriage of Ruth (a Moabite) to Boaz (her Jewish kinsman-redeemer). On top of all that, God places the two of them in the lineage of King David and, subsequently, in the lineage of Jesus Christ. Even though God's name is rarely mentioned directly in the book, you see His providential care as He works through the faithfulness of His people in their everyday lives.

In the Book of Esther, we find larger-than-life characters and storylines with twists and turns. We encounter a defiant queen, a prideful King, a beautiful orphan girl and her devout, protective Uncle, and a vicious villain set on a mission to destroy the Jewish nation. While God's name is never mentioned in the book, there are so many "coincidences" that even the most skeptical reader will finish this historical narrative thinking a higher power must have been in control. A higher power was, and His name is the One True God.

Friend, God is never out of control. Not in the lives of the people we read about in the Bible, and not in your life. The enemy can try to do his worst in your life. He can bring unforeseen circumstances and events you never would have wanted. But God, in His providential care, can turn them all toward a greater and final purpose. God governs all things (Prov. 19:21), directs all things (Eph. 1:11), controls all things (Dan. 4:35), and sustains all things (Col. 1:17).

You may not see it yet, but you can wholeheartedly trust that God allows everything to happen for a reason, from the smallest detail of your life to the greatest. God's plan is loving. God's plan is good. God's plan is purposeful. He will strengthen you. He will help you. He will uphold you (Isa. 41:10). Rest in the hope of His providence.

Two years after Adam's passing, Laurel was still grieving but also moving through life. And while she was regularly telling God, *"I've got this; I'm fine,"* she missed the camaraderie of a marriage partnership. Then, one day, she prayed, "I don't need anybody in my life. I'm totally fine. However, if you do want me to marry somebody, here's my list of expectations. And I kid you not," she said, "pen to paper, I wrote a checklist to God." Little did Laurel know that God was working on her checklist behind the scenes as He brought Matt, a dear friend of 20 years, into the picture. Engaged in three weeks and married three months later, Laurel sits in amazement at God's goodness. "The verse that ties all things together is Ephesians 3:20: 'Now to him who is able to do far more abundantly than all that we ask or think.' God did way more than I thought He was able. I thought I was too old. I thought I was unlovable. I thought I had too much baggage. The word providence literally means the hand of God. And, as I look back through my life, through all the ups and downs, all the mountains and valleys, I see throughout my life that God's hand was in it."

A Closing Prayer

Lord, how thankful I am that you lovingly control all things. Your providence is a reliable source of strength, helping me rest in the knowledge that you are working behind the scenes. Thank you for the many stories in the Bible and in the world around me that show me this truth. Remind me of your providential care in my past so I can wholeheartedly trust you when the unforeseen, unwelcome circumstances arise in my future. Amen.

To listen to Laurel's story, go to www.storytellerslive.org/wherehopemeetsyou and look for "Hope in the Providence of God."

Day 10

Hope in Redemption

"O Israel, hope in the LORD! For with the LORD
there is steadfast love, and with him is plentiful redemption."
—Psalm 130:7

Valerie grew up in a small town and was raised in a family that believed in going to church. It was the quintessential life until the day a man came into her home and attacked her mother and her aunt. "I believe that is the first time fear actually entered me as a little girl," Valerie remembered. Then, only a few years later, Valerie herself was attacked and sexually assaulted. This set off a spiral of thoughts in her. "I was looking at every man as an attacker, every man as somebody who would do harm to me. And I thought that being a lesbian was the way to go." It was a lifestyle Valerie knew her parents wouldn't approve of, so she tried to hide it.

After high school, she married her first husband, but they fought often, which led Valerie to leave. The years that followed took Valerie into a dark world of drugs and prostitution, then divorce and remarriage. Valerie soon had children and tried to stay sober. But, when her second husband went to prison, and she had four kids to care for, the only way she saw out was to rejoin that familiar dark world and sell drugs. "The more you sell, the more you get in that lifestyle," Valerie said. And that lifestyle was hard to leave. Even after three years in prison, a vow to leave the gay lifestyle and quit drugs, and nine months in a halfway house, Valerie went back to old ways, and this time it ended in a 29-year prison sentence. But then, the miraculous happened. One day, while in prison, the Lord spoke to Valerie's heart in a way she couldn't deny. "I was so, so tired. I didn't know at the time where this weariness came from, but it was the Lord letting me know how heavy the sin was that I got myself entangled with. One day, I decided, OK, Lord, I'm done. I can't do this anymore. You just have your way in my life."

Have you ever knelt in prayer for a loved one, but in your heart thought they were too far gone for God to bring redemption to their life? Or perhaps you've sat in judgment of others and thought God shouldn't offer them the gift of redemption. Or, maybe, in your shame and guilt, you adopted the lie that you were too sinful for God to bring redemption to you. The fact is God is in the business of spiritual heart transformation, and no matter what the past holds, every person is a candidate for God's redemption (Rev. 5:9).

Redemption in the Bible means regaining or restoring something that was lost. It comes from the word "redeem," which means to "buy back or buy out." The term was used to describe the idea of buying a slave's freedom back and releasing that slave from their bondage. God has given this rescue offer to anyone who will accept it. He paid for each person's freedom with the blood of His Son, Jesus Christ (Rom. 3:23-24). His desire is for every person to live unenslaved. Redemption is the epicenter of the gospel message.

We see many beautiful stories of redemption in God's Word: Rahab, the Canaanite prostitute turned believer in the one true God and placed in the lineage of Christ (Josh. 2 and 6; Matt. 1:5); Mary Magdalene, the demon-possessed outcast turned follower of Jesus and chosen to be the first to see Him resurrected (Luke 8:1-3; Mark 16:9); and Saul, the persecuting Pharisee turned Paul, the bold Apostle called to be the first missionary for the gospel of Christ (Acts 9:1-31). These are stories of salvation. They are stories of deliverance. They are stories of second chances. They are stories that remind us of God's unfailing love and full redemption, and because of that, we have hope (Psalm 130:7).

Through God's redeeming love, you are free from guilt. Free from shame. Free from the bondage of this world. And you are presented with a new way of living. Romans 6:4 says, "We were buried therefore with him by baptism into death, in order that, just as Christ was raised from the dead by the glory of the Father, we too might walk in newness of life." Redemption offers an escape from the dominion of darkness to the Kingdom of light (Col. 1:13-14). A pilgrimage from old ways and patterns of living to new existence and growth (2 Cor. 5:17). A perspective shift from the temporary to the eternal (1 John 2:17). And, ultimately, a transformation from slave to saint (Romans 6:22). Praise God for His redeeming love today!

As in most redemption stories, Valerie's change wasn't immediate, but as she began taking steps toward the Lord, He started establishing foundational truths in their relationship. "The Lord will show you who you are, in the deepest valley, wherever you find yourself, the Lord will show you who you are," Valerie said. Soon, as she grew in her relationship with the Lord, she began to see her sin and the love of God more clearly. "The Lord was showing me who I was, even in my messed-up state. I said, OK, Lord, whatever you want to do, do it. I began to read my Bible, and the Lord began to talk to me. And whenever He talked to me, I'd write it down. And I'd give it to the ladies in prison." Soon, within the prison walls, Valerie began leading Bible studies and facilitating prayer circles every night. It's those evening prayers that she credits for her early release from prison. After her release, God led Valerie to the position of resident director for a faith-based rehabilitation facility for women. "I can't believe God would choose me. He delivered me from homosexuality. I'm ten years clean, sober, and celibate. Only by the power of God. Just know, if it's your child, if it's your brother, your spouse, whoever it is, God can turn it around because He turned it around for me."

A Closing Prayer

Lord, thank you for your redeeming love and the power of redemption in my life and in the lives of all Believers. Thank you for buying me back through the blood of your Son. Help me to never take the ransom you paid for granted. Today, I pray for those who are choosing to live apart from you, for those who think they are too far gone for you to save them, and for those who think you could never redeem what they have done. Help them to see the need for you in their lives and the love you have for them. Amen.

To listen to Valerie's story, go to www.storytellerslive.org/wherehopemeetsyou and look for "Hope in Redemption."

Day 11

Hope in Faith

"As we look not to the things that are seen but to the things that are unseen. For the things that are seen are transient, but the things that are unseen are eternal."
—2 Corinthians 4:18

Emily's faith had always played an important role in her life, but she saw it as something she did for God, praying only when she needed something. Then, on an unexpected day, she found herself in a dire situation. At her husband's routine colonoscopy, they found cancer, and Emily found herself in a state of shock as Satan whispered every fearful thought imaginable. In the midst of her fear, Emily was desperate. She knew her trust in God needed to be strengthened, so she set out to develop deep roots of faith. Emily began pouring herself into God's Word, putting what she referred to as oil in her lamp. "The lamp was me, and the oil was my faith," Emily said. "This oil of faith was a source of light in my darkness."

Through months of sitting before the Lord, Emily eventually said, "I surrender to you, whatever the outcome, because I know whatever happens, you will be with me." This declaration was a turning point for Emily, and, praise God, her husband was healed. But, just as in life, Emily's whole world stopped again in an instant. She received a call that her daughter had passed away. "What came next was torrential waves of grief. My heart was completely shattered into a million pieces. Satan was trying his best to destroy us, and we were not going to let that happen. We were going to cling to our faith."

For the Christian, faith is confident certainty. It is unwavering hope. It is a guaranteed covenant. It is not wishful thinking, delusional reasoning, or a blind leap. It is an informed assurance that turns the unknown future into a present reality. Faith is boldness. Courage. Strength. Stability. And it stands secure on the rock-solid and trustworthy promises of God and His Word. However, living from this foundation of faith can be difficult, especially in seasons of suffering. You must discipline yourself to see the world through a spiritual lens. How do you do that? You begin by refocusing your eyes.

First, you must make Jesus your center of attention. The perfect illustration of this valuable step is found in the familiar story of Peter walking on the water (Matt. 14:22-33). In this passage, it's clear that if Peter kept his eyes on Jesus, his faith allowed him to do the unimaginable. It was only when his vision got distracted by the winds around him that he began to sink. However, even in that moment, as Peter cried out to Jesus, Jesus reached out His hand and caught him. Keep your eyes focused on Jesus, and what you think is impossible will be possible for you as well.

The second step in seeing the world through a spiritual lens is to focus your eyes on the unseen (2 Cor. 4:18), knowing God is working and fighting on your behalf. Again, a great visual of this concept is found in the story of the servant of the prophet Elisha (2 Kings 6:15-23). Elisha's servant is frightened by the very real army approaching them and surrounding the city. In the physical realm, it appeared that the enemy was going to overtake them. The spiritual realm, however, painted a different picture. Elisha knew this and prayed for his servant, "Then Elisha prayed and said, 'O LORD, please open his eyes that he may see.' So the LORD opened the eyes of the young man, and he saw, and behold, the mountain was full of horses and chariots of fire all around Elisha" (2 Kings 6:17). The Lord was fighting on their behalf in the unseen spiritual realm, and the Lord is fighting for you, too. Focus on the unseen and watch God work.

Finally, your spiritual vision is developed by looking intently into the Word of God. After all, the Apostle Paul tells us that faith itself originates there (Rom. 10:17). The Word of God helps you see, illuminating your path and directing your footsteps (Ps. 119:105; 133). The Word of God increases the prescription of your spiritual lens as it enlightens the eyes of your heart to the hope to which He has called you (Eph. 1:17-18). And the Word of God consistently works to help you see your actions and thoughts more clearly (Heb. 4:12). Read God's Word every day, and your eyesight will become crystal clear.

Putting these three disciplines into practice is a constant choice you face daily. Do you place your hope in this world, or do you place your hope in faith? One will leave you disappointed, disillusioned, and dissatisfied, while the other will leave you comforted, encouraged, and content. Keep your eyes on the prize and make faith your focus.

As Emily's nightmare of losing her daughter became reality, she knew she must completely rely on God. "We had no other option but to trust God to carry us through this." So, she began speaking God's Word over her life, reminding herself that this world was not her home. "Our true citizenship is in heaven," she reminded herself, "and God will not leave us or abandon us." Through her foundation of faith, she chose to praise God in the midst of her pain. "Some days were harder than others, but I kept taking steps forward. I kept believing in God's goodness and His love for me, and I kept trusting in Him to lead me out of this darkness. Our family's faith in God held us together."

Today, Emily is still choosing faith over her fears. Through this spiritual lens, she has learned that while God doesn't create suffering, He has the power to redeem it and turn it into a thing of beauty meant to be treasured. In her words, her faith tells her that "God sees the bigger picture of life, and it is beautiful."

A Closing Prayer

Lord, thank you for being the Author and Perfecter of my faith (Heb. 12:2) and the solid foundation on which I stand. Thank you for the gift of spiritual insight. I pray you will continue to open the eyes of my heart to your purpose for my life and to your unseen glory. I will forever trust you completely, knowing you are fighting on my behalf.

To listen to Emily's story, go to www.storytellerslive.org/wherehopemeetsyou and look for "Hope in Faith."

Day 12

Hope In Heartbreak

"The LORD is near to the brokenhearted
and saves the crushed in spirit."
—Psalm 34:18

When Kelly was in high school, something happened that sent her on a perpetual cycle of shame and sweeping things under the rug. As she got older, Kelly continued to fight her feelings of not being good enough, and her mental health only worsened when her husband began struggling with opioid addiction. Kelly tried helping her husband. She tried controlling the situation. She tried hiding all that was happening behind closed doors. "I put up this facade that everything was perfect, and we were great," Kelly said. Years went by, and things just got worse.

In order for her marriage to have a fighting chance, Kelly knew she needed to work on herself, so she began therapy and counseling and pursuing her relationship with the Lord. However, eventually she found out her husband was having an affair on top of his addiction. Her heart was broken. *She* was broken. "I didn't know what else to do," Kelly said. "I knew my marriage was over. And, as I was on my knees, asking God what to do, I felt arms wrapped around my body, and I just stayed there on the floor crying. I knew God was holding me, and He was going to be there for me."

What happens when someone you love betrays you? How do you live hope-filled amidst feelings of anger, resentment, bitterness, and intense grief? What do you do when your "happily ever after" ends, and you are left heartbroken? Because we were created for connection and because we live in a fallen world, these are questions many of us have had to struggle with at some point in our lives. As 1980s rocker Pat Benatar once sang, love can in fact be a battlefield. After all, there is a reason the saying "all's fair in love and war" has become a slogan for shattered relationships and hearts.

Jesus Himself knew the feelings of betrayal and heartbreak first-hand. When Judas Iscariot sealed His death (with a kiss, of all things) in the Garden of Gethsemane (Matt. 26:48-50), there is no doubt Jesus, in His humanity, experienced the deep pangs of relational rejection. Then, while Jesus was held in the High Priest's courtyard, being questioned and falsely accused, one of His closest disciples, Peter, denied even knowing Him (Matt. 26:69-75). Even though Jesus had predicted this denial, there must have been a sense of sorrow within Him as Peter blatantly dismissed Him as a Teacher and a Friend. Jesus knew the depths of rejection unlike anything you or I can or will experience as He willingly hung on the cross for those who profoundly mistreated Him, all the while forgiving them for their horrific acts. Talk about humility within heartbreak!

How did Jesus endure such emotional suffering? Scripture is clear. It wasn't easy. We are told Jesus prayed and pleaded with

God, offering fervent cries and tears in the Garden (Heb. 5:7). But Jesus also knew His betrayal, denial, and heartbreak were part of a much larger plan and a beautiful, beyond-happy ending. Did it make it easier? Absolutely not. But Jesus trusted that the Father's will would be done, and He also wholeheartedly knew the day of healing would eventually come.

If you've gone through heartbreak (or maybe you are experiencing it now), you've undoubtedly been told time will heal you. And while yes, it can, the statement is only partly true. God alone fully "heals the brokenhearted and binds up their wounds" (Psalm 147:3). Relying on Him for true comfort and healing is essential. Go to Him in prayer. Pour your heart out to Him. Cry and yell and plead. But then remind yourself of who you are. You are His child (John 1:12). His special possession (1 Pet. 2:9). His masterpiece (Eph.2:10). His beloved bride (Isaiah 62:5). He can and will bring you back to "happily ever after" one day. Trust in His timing and His plan for your life.

Relationships are worth rejoicing over. Marriages are worth celebrating. But the only relationship that will perfectly fulfill you, save you, and bring you joyful contentment is your relationship with Christ. Spend time relishing in His love for you today and tether your heart to His.

Ultimately, Kelly filed for divorce from her husband, but she continued to feel the pursuing love of the Father as she surrendered to His plans. "I love the verse, the Lord is close to the brokenhearted and saves the crushed in spirit. I was so broken. I felt like I had lost half my body. I had to grieve my marriage." Kelly knew the Lord wanted her to depend solely on Him, so she began discovering who she was in Christ. "I was continuing to lean into God, and I knew that if I trusted Him, good things would come."

Looking back, Kelly can see God's providential hand holding her, and she sits in thankfulness, knowing God will continue to carry her and her children. "I wouldn't know God like I do if I didn't go through what had happened. He gave me the resilience and made me who I am because He knew I could do it. It is the pain, and the heartbreak, and the sadness that brought me to the Lord. We may not have a happy ending, but we are happy."

A Closing Prayer

Lord, I thank you for being a Father whose desire is to be in a relationship with me. Thank you for loving, accepting, and approving of me, and because of that, I am enough. While I praise you for the gifts of friendship and marriage, help me to place my relationship with you above all else. And Lord, when heartbreak inevitably comes into my life, help me to put my hope in you and live from humility and forgiveness as Jesus modeled to me. It is in His name I ask for these things. Amen.

To listen to Kelly's story, go to www.storytellerslive.org/wherehopemeetsyou and look for "Hope in Heartbreak."

Day 13

Hope in Addiction

"For freedom Christ has set us free; stand firm therefore, and do not submit again to a yoke of slavery."
—Galatians 5:1

Growing up with an alcoholic father and in a performance-based family culture, Kristy learned early on how to function among secrets and never ask for help. "Secrets keep us sick," Kristy reflected, "and I carried a lot of secrets for a long time." As she got older, the pressures of performing and the heaviness of her secrets led Kristy down a path of numbness, and "alcohol did the trick." It became a friend to her that she would turn to on and off for more than thirty years. "I would justify my drinking in so many ways," Kristy said. "I had no idea of the power that that substance had over me."

Over those decades, Kristy continued performing and pretending for people's approval. She married her college sweetheart, had three children, wore busyness like a badge of honor, and became an expert at caretaking and controlling. Then, the day came when Kristy recognized her son struggling with alcohol as well, and she knew she had to face herself. "The light had gone out in him, and sadly it had gone out in me too." Soon after this revelation, Kristy and her husband checked her son into rehab, and a little over three months later, Kristy's husband checked her in as well.

Addiction does not discriminate. It's one of the most prevalent problems facing our culture today. And it's a disease that can destroy lives, relationships, and dreams. But amidst the pain and sorrow, there is hope, as God is an agent of change. He can heal the deepest of wounds and break the most binding chains of addiction.

In chapters 7 and 8 of the book of Romans, the Apostle Paul gives a dissertation that we can all relate to (as we are all sinners). It is incredibly applicable for bringing hope to the addict (no matter what that addiction may be). In these chapters, Paul refers to the struggle of sin as well as the gift of the Spirit. In reference to his sin, Paul says, "For I do not understand my own actions. For I do not do what I want, but I do the very thing I hate" (Rom. 7:15). Oh, how we all can relate!

Then, Paul goes on to say, "For I know that nothing good dwells in me, that is, in my flesh. For I have the desire to do what is right, but not the ability to carry it out. For I do not do the good I want, but the evil I do not want is what I keep on doing" (vs. 18-19). Does that sound familiar? As Paul reflects on his choices of living, he continues by saying that while he delights in God's law, he also sees another law at work within him, the law of sin, which is making him a prisoner to himself. Paul writes, "Wretched man that I am! Who will deliver me from this body of death?" (v.24).

Paul is completely worn out from his unsuccessful efforts to overcome his sinful nature. And, if we stopped reading here, we would all be hopelessly paralyzed. But Paul doesn't leave us there. As he is overwhelmed by a sense of powerlessness, he comes to realize his need for redemption through Christ. Keep in mind, before this shift of thinking, Paul referred to himself nearly 40 times! He was self-focused, self-obsessed, and self-deprecating. But in verse 25, he turns his mind to Jesus and says, "Thanks be to God through Jesus Christ our Lord! So then, I myself serve the law of God with my mind, but with my flesh I serve the law of sin." Then, as Paul begins chapter 8, his focus is now on the truths found in Jesus, truths like: there is no condemnation in Christ; you are set free through the Spirit; as a child of God the power of the Spirit resides in you and gives you life; you are no longer a slave to sin; and you are a co-heir with Christ (v. 1-17). These are fighting words, especially in the face of addiction.

Friend, while the passions of the flesh wage war against your soul (1 Pet. 2:11), God offers you victory and freedom (Gal. 5:1). Your job is to surrender, recognize your powerlessness, and exalt in God's power. Approach His throne of grace with confidence, so that you may receive mercy and find grace to help you in your time of need (Heb. 4:16). And, if someone you love is struggling with drugs or alcohol, do not despair. You serve a Father who is greater. His grace can and will provide a path of freedom, healing, and lasting change. Believe it today.

It took Kristy eleven months to realize that her addiction was undermining her worth and value. "You know, alcohol had just totally blocked me from the sunlight of the Spirit," she said. "It had totally blocked me from who I was and who God intended me to be." Through God's love and her family's love, Kristy began to find healing. She began to face the things in her life she had been running from all those years, and the things she was running to as a result.

God began teaching her in powerful ways, letting her know He was fighting on her behalf. "I serve a God who saved me out of addiction and brought me back up. God always reminds me every day that I am His special possession. Being an alcoholic has been the hardest and best gift to me. The stigma of addiction does not get the final say; my God does. And, He says, 'Kristy, you're not defined to me by being an alcoholic but by being my daughter who I love, and I died for so that you could walk in full freedom.' I am forever grateful to walk out the rest of my days holding His right hand very tightly because none of us were ever meant to do this life on our own."

A Closing Prayer

Lord, addiction looms around every corner of my life, disguised in many ways. Help me to see my sins and surrender my addictions to you. Thank you for being an agent of change. Thank you for fighting my battles and offering me victory in places where I feel helpless, hopeless, and defeated. I offer up my body and my mind to your power today. Amen.

To listen to Kristy's story, go to www.storytellerslive.org/wherehopemeetsyou and look for "Hope in Addiction."

Day 14

Hope in Forgiveness

"Be kind to one another, tenderhearted,
forgiving one another, as God in Christ forgave you."
—Ephesians 4:32

At the age of six, Jane unexpectedly lost her mother. It was a time of confusion for her, a time of questioning God, and a time of feeling different. All she craved was normalcy in her life. Ten years later, her father remarried, and a tumultuous relationship with her stepmother began. "She was really critical," Jane recalled, "and a little seed of bitterness started forming in my heart."

Over the years, the seed of bitterness grew as Jane's stepmother continued to make hurtful comments and decisions. But Jane now had a husband and a family of her own, and she was trying to focus on them. Then, the day came when her father passed away, and, as they were going over documents, they noticed her stepmother had transferred her father's largest asset into her name. This realization came in the middle of Jane's family being in a financial crisis as well. "The fear, the anxiety, the worry just took over. And then, all of a sudden, that inheritance that was rightfully mine took on a whole new meaning, rehearsing every hurt, every injury, every insult that I'd ever had from the hands of my stepmother."

Jane and her siblings soon filed a lawsuit, and she continued nursing her grudge, almost consumed by it. Then, through the innocence of a child, God began a work in Jane's heart, and conviction set in. "The Bible calls us to love our enemies and forgive, but I couldn't. I would put off bitterness, and then put it back on. I would pray, Lord, please help me to forgive, but then I would also pray, Lord, please help me win the lawsuit."

Ultimately, Jane lost the lawsuit, and God brought her to the end of herself. She realized she had been trying hard to conjure up forgiveness on her own. She thought about how God had dealt with her own sin and selfishness, and God began refocusing her eyes. "God took my eyes off my stepmother in her sin, in her meanness, in her selfishness, and put the focus on me. And I saw my meanness, my selfishness, my wrong as I never had before. I have no right to judge, and that took me to my knees."

Forgiveness is one of the most powerful acts a follower of Christ can do to show the love of our Father in Heaven. There is something incredibly compelling about seeing someone who has been terribly wronged say, "I forgive you" to the offender. It's as if you can feel the Holy Spirit palpably at work in the victim, showing the love, compassion, and kindness of Jesus.

Oftentimes, we think forgiveness is just for the offender, but God is clear that forgiveness is for us as well. It connects you more deeply with God. It humbles you as you recognize the price Jesus paid for your sin. It allows you to experience His power working through you. And it enables you to move past bitterness, hurt, and resentment. Forgiveness is an integral part of salvation and of the Christian life.

In Matthew 18:21, Peter asks Jesus how many times he should forgive his brother or sister who sins against him. And before Jesus answers, Peter throws out a hopeful question: "up to seven times?" Peter was expecting to sound extremely loving because, according to Jewish rabbis of the day, three times was the accepted number of forgiveness offers. However, Jesus' reply stunned Peter as He said, "I do not say to you seven times, but seventy-seven times" (v. 22). This was not a math problem Jesus was giving to His disciples. He didn't literally mean you forgive 77 times and at 78 you don't. No, this response was Jesus' way of saying you are to forgive your offender an unlimited number of times. Jesus could have easily followed up His answer with, "much like I have forgiven you."

Jesus is the ultimate example of forgiveness, and He expects His followers to uphold this standard of grace as well. In Scripture, you are told to "be kind to one another, tenderhearted, forgiving one another, as God in Christ forgave you" (Eph. 4:32), and to "[bear] with one another and, if one has a complaint against another, forgiving each other; as the Lord has forgiven you, so you also must forgive" (Col 3:13). As a follower of Christ, you forgive out of love, obedience, and gratefulness to God. You forgive out of the overflow of Jesus' forgiveness to you.

Today, you may need to offer forgiveness in a small manner. Maybe your spouse snapped at you, maybe your child was unappreciative, or maybe a friend didn't include you. Can you take a moment and tell the Lord you forgive them and let it go? Or, perhaps, you have a deep-rooted hurt that has been manifesting bitterness and resentment over the years, and you think, there is no way I can offer up forgiveness. And, you can't. But God can. He can help you move forward with forgiveness. Remember, it's a choice, not a feeling. Feelings will come later. Just take one step of forgiveness right now and allow the Lord to do a work in your heart.

When God refocused Jane's eyes on her own sin, she soon realized "I was not the spotless hero of my story, and my stepmother was not the villain. And it was crushing, but it was also strangely freeing because with repentance came forgiveness. I didn't have to try. My grudge just deflated and disappeared with that knowledge."

As Jane let go of the bitterness she had harbored for so many years and started forgiving her stepmother, God also began opening her eyes to His blessings and faithfulness. "In the moment that He was showing me how I was worse than I think I am, I also saw that I am so loved and so known. And His faithfulness just washed over me in the most incredible way." Today, Jane says she continues to practice forgiveness and giving thanks for her blessings. She remains overwhelmingly grateful for the Lord's pursuit of her and her unforgiving heart, and for bringing her to a saving faith.

A Closing Prayer

Father, I don't have the words to tell you how thankful I am that you have freely forgiven me. Thank you for the price that was paid in Jesus' death on the cross to offer me that forgiveness. Help me to live from a stance of freely forgiving others. When people wrong me, disappoint me, or hurt me, help me to lean into your Holy

Spirit and allow its power to do a work within my heart. Today, Lord, I choose forgiveness out of my love, gratefulness, and obedience to you. Amen.

To listen to Jane's story, go to www.storytellerslive.org/wherehopemeetsyou and look for "Hope in Forgiveness."

Day 15

Hope in Depression

"But you, God, see the trouble of the afflicted;
you consider their grief and take it in hand."
—Psalm 10:14 (NIV)

As a child, Patti grew up in an environment of physical, psychological, and sexual abuse that continued into her adult years. As a result, she developed a pattern of staying quiet and trying to please others. It was a pattern that led Patti into a devastating season of depression. At 49, she was hit with one heartache after another. "I felt like I'd been under this avalanche, and I couldn't catch my breath," Patti remembered. Dealing with this period of unimaginable pressures and trying to work as a women's ministry director began to weigh heavily on Patti. "It was taking its toll," she said. "To be depressed means you are hard pressed. I was hard pressed. Depression had come and settled on me so heavily that I thought I was having a heart attack."

The physical symptoms of Patti's depression ultimately manifested themselves to a point where she couldn't sleep, and it was tormenting. In desperation, Patti cried out to the Lord, and He sweetly answered her, telling her of the ways she had been believing lies about herself, finding confidence in people rather than Him, and looking for safety in the things of this world rather than His loving arms. "I was looking at my depression through the physical and emotional, but this episode was very spiritual. And my spirit acknowledged the truth." In the days that came, the Lord continued to work on Patti's heart, telling her, "I have not given you a spirit of fear or dread, disability or discouragement. Rather, I have made a way for you to gain victory," Patti heard the Lord say. "You must rise up and defeat the enemy of your soul."

There is a long list of factors in life that can lead us down the dark road of depression: fear, comparison, hopelessness, loss, and illness, just to name a few. The stresses and pressures of this world can become so incredibly overwhelming that the clouds begin to overshadow the sun. If we aren't intentional in fighting it through the power of God, our light can go out. However, there is hope amidst the heaviness. There is peace amidst the pain. There is deliverance amidst the distress. There is a Savior amidst the sorrow. His name is Jesus, and He is with you. He sees you, and He hears your cries.

Oftentimes, when depression sweeps into our lives, it brings with it many "friends." One of its most frequent companions is its friend "loneliness." There is nothing the enemy wants more in a season of suffering than for you to feel alone. It is a lie that seems to attach like glue, and you must claim truth over it. God tells you, "fear not, for I am with you; be not dismayed, for I am your God; I will strengthen you, I will help you, I will uphold you with my righteous right hand" (Isaiah 41:10). God will never leave you or forsake you (Heb. 13:5). He is with you in your depression.

While loneliness tends to be depression's best friend, other companions that often accompany it are "overlooked" and "dismissed." When your sorrow becomes suffocating, you feel as if you aren't seen. Your pain and struggles feel invisible to the world, and your depression worsens. However, the truth is, you are seen by the Creator of the world. It is the nature of God's character to observe, recognize, and notice you. One of the many Hebrew names for God is *El Roi*, "the God who sees me." You are never hidden from God's sight. He sees you in your depression.

Depression's final accomplice is named "unheard," and, in a time of intense sorrow, it can make you feel completely hopeless. You feel as if no one understands, no one cares, no one wants to listen. But, again, that is another lie from the enemy. God hears your cries and listens to you in your pain. The psalms are full of reminders of God's listening ear: "In my distress I called upon the LORD; to my God I cried for help. From his temple he heard my voice, and my cry to him reached his ears" (Psalm 18:6); "When the righteous cry for help, the LORD hears and delivers them out of all their troubles" (Psalm 34:17); "Evening and morning and at noon I utter my complaint and moan, and he hears my voice" (Psalm 55:17). God is always available, giving attention to your prayers. He hears you in your depression.

God is with you. He sees you. He hears you. Tuck these truths deep into your soul for those days when the clouds seem to be heavy in your heart, and the enemy is coming at you with his army and his lies. Depression doesn't have to have the final say in your life. Inhale the hope of God today and let Him have the final word.

As the Lord laid His truths on Patti's heart, she began to feel His strength, and she recognized she wasn't fighting this battle of depression alone. She had His power on her side, and He soon brought 36 prayer warriors into her life. For over a month, these women came to Patti's house, spoke God's Word over her, and lavished her with His love. "The healing words of these women changed my life," Patti said. "And, I've been walking free and liberated from depression for 19 years now. These women came with God's love, His purpose, and His empowerment."

As Patti reflects on those days, she sees purpose in the anguish she experienced. "I found a new respect for people suffering from depression. I can't tell you how it happened, but I know that when my weak heart came in contact with God's strong heart, I gained strength. God took the hopelessness out of depression, and I was pressed into knowing no other helper but God."

A Closing Prayer

God, thank you that even depression bows down to you. When I am overwhelmed by this world and sadness begins to creep into my life, help me remember that you are with me, that you see me, and that you hear me. Father, silence the lies of the enemy and increase the volume of your truths. Thank you, Lord, that depression doesn't win. You have the final say in my life, and for that, I am blessed. Amen.

To listen to Patti's story, go to www.storytellerslive.org/wherehopemeetsyou and look for "Hope In Depression."

Day 16

Hope in Loss

"So we are always of good courage. We know that while
we are at home in the body we are away from the Lord,
for we walk by faith, not by sight. Yes, we are of good courage,
and we would rather be away from the body
and at home with the Lord."
—2 Corinthians 5:6–8

Raised in a family whose foundation was Jesus, Kara was taught from an early age, "The blessing of Jesus is just that: Jesus. And, the blessing of God is that He sent Jesus. That is the blessing." It was a foundation that shaped her own family as she married and had three children. By her early 40s, Kara was content and happy, but she felt God drawing her closer to Him. She wanted to know and experience more of God, so she began pouring herself into Him and His Word. Little did she know that God was preparing her for what was to come: two storms she never could have imagined.

The first storm was her husband's diagnosis with lymphoma, and while it was a hard season, the Lord ultimately healed him. And, the experience left in its wake a deeper faith for her, and especially for her middle son, Cooper. Then, only a few months later, a storm came that had the possibility of tearing her world apart. She received a call from her husband that Cooper was in an ATV accident. As she rushed home, her husband was waiting for her in the front yard. She opened the car door, and he said Cooper was gone. "It's like your mind can't even process what someone's telling you. So, I started saying, 'God is good. He is faithful. God is still good.' And I was just screaming that in my front yard." Kara knew deep in her heart that she had to find Jesus in that moment.

Horatio Spafford was a Presbyterian layman, a successful lawyer, and a real estate broker in Chicago in the late 1800s, and he knew all too well the weight of loss. He lost his four-year-old son to scarlet fever. He lost much of his fortune in the Chicago Fire of 1871. And then, two years later, his four remaining daughters were killed in a terrible ship collision while crossing the Atlantic Ocean for a vacation to Europe. His wife, who had survived the wreck, sent a telegram from England to Horatio saying, "Saved alone . . . what shall I do?" Horatio immediately got on a ship to go and be with his wife.

During Horatio's trip to England, the ship's captain informed him that they were passing over the spot where his daughters had passed away. In that moment, in his pain and grief, Horatio took to pen and paper and wrote the lines of the famous hymn, "It Is Well with My Soul." The first stanza he penned said, "When peace like a river attendeth my way, when sorrows like sea billows roll; whatever my lot, thou hast taught me to say, 'It is well, it is well, with my soul.'" These eloquent and comforting words we still sing today were a testament to Horatio's faith, trust, and hope amid indescribable loss.

Hope in loss. It seems like an impossible, unreasonable, and preposterous thought. However, it is exactly what Jesus wants you to experience in the midst of a loved one's passing. He wants you to be comforted, knowing death is not the end. It is a transition to Heaven, where "He will wipe away every tear from their eyes, and death shall be no more, neither shall there be mourning, nor crying, nor pain anymore, for the former things have passed away" (Rev. 21:4). Because of Jesus' death and resurrection, you have hope.

Keep in mind that hope does not mean you won't suffer loss. To grieve is to be human. Jesus Himself wept after the passing of his friend Lazarus (John 11:35). And while He knew that Lazarus' death would ultimately glorify His Father in Heaven, Jesus' tears also flowed from the sorrow of His friends around Him. In His divine nature, Jesus knew life wasn't supposed to be this way, but in His human nature, He felt the immense pain of loss and grief. When you are suffering from the death of someone you love, rest in knowing Jesus understands and grieves alongside you.

The Apostle Paul tells us that, as Christians, we grieve, but not like the rest of humankind, who have no hope (1 Thess. 4:13). Our sorrow is a temporary sadness. Jesus' death and resurrection are proof of that. For the Believer, death is not the end. It is the beginning of eternity, where you are present with the Father in a far more glorious place. This is what brings us peace. This is what provides us strength. This is what gives us hope and allows us to say, "It is well, it is well, with my soul."

In the days, weeks, and months after Cooper's passing, Kara gained much insight into God's faithfulness, strength, and love.

"You can find Him in the middle of your storm. You can find Him after your storm. You can find Him. He's always there. There *is* hope amidst suffering." And, as Kara processed the pain of her loss, the Lord sweetly gave her visions and Scripture to hold onto.

The first vision the Lord gave was of Kara laying her head on His chest as He comforted her with His promise found in 2 Corinthians 5:8 that when we're absent from the body, we are present with the Lord. Next, the Lord gave Kara a vision of Cooper standing with Jesus. "I'm behind him," Kara said. "And Jesus put His arm around Cooper and motioned, like it's time to go. And Cooper looked at him, and he said, 'Wait, I've got to tell my mom that I'm OK.' I know beyond a shadow of a doubt where Cooper is right now."

Finally, while on a mission trip to Cambodia, the Lord continued to shift Kara's eyes toward Heaven, as one of the men living there had painted a portrait of Jesus and Cooper. It was the exact vision the Lord had given Kara of the two of them together! "Cooper was never built for this earth, and neither are we," Kara reflected. "We are here for a while, and we are here for a purpose, but eternity is what we're built for. So, I try to keep my eyes on what is coming, and not what is gone. And, I have learned that you can live with suffering and with grief and with sadness, and, in the very same breath, have joy. I promise you, you can."

A Closing Prayer

Heavenly Father, thank you for hope amid loss and death here on earth. Thank you for the gift of knowing loved ones who have passed are now present with you, and I will see them again. Prepare me with your promises so that my eyes shift toward you when mortality is mentioned. Thank you to Jesus, who through His death and resurrection, overcame death for me. Amen

To listen to Kara's story, go to www.storytellerslive.org/wherehopemeetsyou and look for "Hope in Loss."

Day 17

Hope in a Diagnosis

"May the God of hope fill you with all joy and peace in believing, so that by the power of the Holy Spirit you may abound in hope."
—Romans 15:13

In 2019, God gave Leslie the word "celebrate" as her word of the year; birthdays, holidays, weddings, graduations, births, she was going to celebrate big! Then, September came, and a lump in her breast changed everything. "My mind just went to all the scary places and all the what ifs," Leslie recalled. But then she thought, "If I believe what I say I believe, I've got to trust Him. I choose to trust Him. I knew God's ways were higher than my ways. And, I know that He's sovereign in everything and that everything is sifted through His hands." Two weeks later, her results came in, and she headed to her doctor. "I'll never forget, he walked in with his nurse, he tenderly walked over to me, put his arm around me, and said, 'It's breast cancer.'"

Leslie knew in her heart that it was, and she prepared herself for treatment. Sixteen weeks of chemotherapy, then surgery, then radiation, all of which brought many challenges into her life. She experienced nausea, bone pain, headaches, sores, and blisters. But in the middle of her pain and suffering, Leslie never felt closer to the Lord. "He is a God who sees me. He knows me. He loves me," she said. "As the chemo progressed, I felt weaker and weaker and sicker and sicker, but I felt so much closer to the Lord, and that was a blessing, that intimacy with the Lord. I learned to trust God in the characteristics of God and not in my circumstances."

Many of us live in fear of a diagnosis. Whether it's cancer or chronic back pain, Alzheimer's or arthritis, diabetes or heart disease, the first response we often have is fear. Our minds get ahead of our bodies, and we worry about the "what ifs," instead of practicing the presence of the Lord, resting in His character, and listening to His voice. We position ourselves in a place of panic rather than positioning ourselves for the Lord's purpose. The enemy loves this.

There is nothing that pleases the enemy more than to try to steal, kill, and destroy you and the life in which you live. After all, that is his mission. He sends his thieves and robbers, and they attack you through deception, distorting God's truth, making you doubt the power and goodness of the Lord. They want to take your life. But the Bible says that Jesus came that you might have life and have it abundantly (John 10:10).

The original Greek word for abundant in this verse is *perissos*, and it carries with it the connotation of a "surplus," an "over and above" what you could ever expect or imagine. God can supply all your needs according to His riches and glory in Christ Jesus (Phil. 4:19). He wants to "fill you with all joy and peace in believing, so that by the power of the Holy Spirit you may abound in hope" (Rom. 15:13). This doesn't mean life will always be comfortable, easy, or long-lived. It means Jesus alone will satisfy, and when you trust His plan and purposes for your life, contentment, serenity, and rejoicing settle in, even amid an unwanted diagnosis.

Jesus desires nothing more than for you to silence the lies of the enemy and his cohorts and listen only to His voice, the shepherd's voice. He knows that is the only way to live an abundant life. In the verses just before John 10:10, Jesus used the illustration of a shepherd leading and caring for his sheep. He spoke about knowing his sheep by name and calling for them. Jesus knew His listeners would know that sheep are experts at discerning their shepherd's voice. They instinctively know his voice, and when he calls, they come running. Jesus wanted His followers (and you) to recognize the importance of distinguishing His voice from the voices of the thieves and robbers. He wants His call to be the only one you follow because He knows it is where you will find safety, security, and protection (John 10:3-9).

So, whether you are living in a season of blessed health or waiting for test results to come or walking through a diagnosis of your own, magnify His name today as the giver of abundant life. Know that He is with you, guiding you along the way. Listen closely for the shepherd's voice. Look for His purpose in your pain. Find hope in His presence. And let His peace, which transcends all understanding, guard your heart and mind in Christ Jesus (Phil. 4:7).

Ultimately, the Lord healed Leslie of her cancer, and she was determined not to waste her journey. She began praying, "Lord, what do you want me to do with this?" The Lord led Leslie to begin reading the journal she had kept throughout her diagnosis and treatment. And as she read, she began reflecting on all the times she received flowers from loved ones. So, she asked, "Lord, are you telling me to do something with flowers?" These questions took Leslie down a road that still blesses people today.

Leslie started a ministry called "Hope Blooms," where she repurposes wedding flowers and takes them to hospitals, funerals, memorials, and even parties. Through her diagnosis, Leslie has seen firsthand how the Lord can take anything and use it for His glory. "It wasn't fun. I don't want to do it again. But I wouldn't change what I learned on the journey and what I learned about God and His character and Who He is to me."

A Closing Prayer

Lord, thank you for being my good shepherd and for providing me with abundant life. Help me to look and listen to you when I am, or a loved one is, diagnosed with a chronic illness or disease. Silence my fears and take my thoughts captive to you. I trust your plan for my life and the lives of those I love, and I will rest in your purpose for them. Amen.

To listen to Leslie's story, go to www.storytellerslive.org/wherehopemeetsyou and look for "Hope in a Diagnosis."

Day 18

Hope in Insecurity

"I praise you, for I am fearfully and wonderfully made. Wonderful are your works; my soul knows it very well."
—Psalm 139:14

Courtney was born with a Type A personality. From a young age, she preferred order, craved control, and worried over a litany of things. Her insecurities only heightened when her parents divorced while she was in second grade. "I barely spoke for an entire year. My stomach hurt all the time from worry," Courtney recalled. Then, around the same time, Courtney heard the gospel message, but the enemy distorted the truth. "I misconstrued the message to be that God would love me and accept me if I proved myself worthy of Him." As a result, Courtney committed herself to living a "perfect" life. She was determined to be good enough for God. But, like all of us, she would inevitably fail. Try and fail. Try and fail.

After riding this roller coaster for years, Courtney soon began believing the lie that she herself was, in fact, a failure. "I was left feeling woefully inadequate of His love," Courtney recalled. "I was exhausted and weary, worn down from the roller coaster, the highs of riding on my own self-righteousness and the lows of plummeting into the depths of my failure and unworthiness."

Then, as a young adult, God gave Courtney a clear picture of His grace through the sacrifice of Jesus. It gave her such hope in her insecurities that she began to ponder a new way of living and asked herself, "What if I laid down my burdens at His feet? What if I surrendered and quit trying to be good enough for Him and rested in the fact that only He is enough?" These were questions that allowed God to begin etching the truths of His grace into Courtney's heart.

We are all capable of feeling insecure from time to time. It's the invisible friend you often unknowingly let into your life at a young age. As you get older, if you don't find your identity in Christ and in who He says you are, that childhood visitor can make his home in your heart, leaving you living in a world of comparison, striving for significance, and searching for acceptance. God does not want you in this world. He wants you to live securely in the truths of who you are as a child of the King.

First, you are valuable, and you were created for a greater purpose. The Lord knit you together in your mother's womb, and you are fearfully and wonderfully made (Psalm 139:13-14). Everything about you is perfect in God's eyes. You are not a mistake. You are not an accident. You are His masterpiece created to do good works, which God has prepared you in advance to do (Eph. 2:10). And, because of that, you are extremely valuable! The fuel that feeds insecurity is the desire to be valued in the eyes of others. The problem with this is that people were never meant to fully satisfy their self-worth. Affirmations and accolades from the world may feel good in the moment, but only the realization of how deeply treasured you are by your Heavenly Father will leave you with true joy and contentment.

Secondly, you are a child of God, chosen by the King, and lavished by His love (1 John 3:1). This position is 100% completely secure through the blood of Christ. There is nothing you can do to earn God's love. He gives it to you freely. There is nothing you can do to take away His love. God sees all your weaknesses and flaws and loves you just the same. Through Jesus, you are holy and righteous before His eyes, and He wants you to live from this place of power.

Finally, you are fully accepted and fully enough. You don't need to prove your self-worth to God. Oftentimes, insecurity tries to pass itself off as humility, but when you take a closer look, insecurity has much more in common with pride than one cares to admit. The two may seem like opposites, but they both stem from very similar roots. Both are self-focused. Both are centered around self-image. Both tempt you to compare yourself to others. Both are searching for validation from others. Both are "flesh" motivated. And, "whoever sows to please their flesh, from the flesh will reap destruction" (Galatians 6:8). Don't let insecurity destroy you!

When you live from a place of insecurity, you are living from a place of disqualification. You are disqualifying who you are in Christ. You are valuable. Chosen. Loved. Holy. Righteous. Accepted. Enough. Let your security be based on who God says you are. This is the only foundation that will stand firm when the floods of insecurity begin to rise (Luke 6:47-49). So, ask yourself, "Has insecurity made its home in my heart? Am I living for the world or for God? Can I surrender my insecurities to the Father and believe I am who He says I am?" Bring your insecurities before God today and let them dissolve into His perfect love.

As Courtney grew closer to the Lord, He began opening her eyes to how her insecurities were manifesting and growing. "God has shown me that there is deep joy and peace in seeking to run the race of this life with a perspective of doing it for Him and no one else," Courtney said. "And, when I run for Him alone, the fear of not being good enough, the fear of how I'll measure up when I compare myself to others, is replaced with freedom."

While Courtney still considers herself a work in progress, she can now embrace her insecurities by accepting her incompleteness. When asked what she would tell her younger self if she could, she said, "I have so much empathy for that little girl. I would tell her, 'You're so afraid of being incomplete, of not being enough, but guess what? You are incomplete because God made you that way, so that you would need Him. He's right here, ready to welcome you into His arms. He is perfectly complete and perfectly enough. And you belong to Him, beloved daughter of the King.'"

A Closing Prayer

Father, thank you that I am your chosen child, dearly loved and accepted. Help me find my self-worth in you alone. When my insecurities rear their ugly heads, refocus my eyes on who you say I am: holy, righteous, valuable, and wonderfully made. Forgive me, Lord, when I look around this world and compare myself to others. And give me the wisdom to live from the secure, solid foundation of your Word alone. Amen.

To listen to Courtney's story, go to www.storytellerslive.org/wherehopemeetsyou and look for "Hope in Insecurity."

Day 19

Hope in Mental Illness

"We destroy arguments and every lofty opinion
raised against the knowledge of God,
and take every thought captive to obey Christ."
—2 Corinthians 10:5

Aimee battled mental illness for most of her adult life. From extreme anxiety and fear to paranoia and delusional visions, Aimee despised how her mind would work. "I was so ashamed. I was a Christian, and bad things weren't supposed to happen to me. I thought I was doing all the right things and that God had allowed this. I was so confused." After multiple stays in psychiatric hospitals, Aimee was eventually diagnosed with schizophrenia. Doctors put her on medication, and it helped, but the shame of her mental illness was so much that she would always stop taking them.

Each time Aimee took herself off the medications, the delusions would start back. Finally, after a month-long stay in the psychiatric hospital, Aimee knew she needed to accept her diagnosis and the treatment her body needed. "Somehow, I realized that I had a true medical condition that was causing all of this. Every time I took the two pills, I'd stay out of the hospital. And every time I went off them, my mind was so fragile that it literally broke. This realization began to change the trajectory of my life. Instead of expecting healing from the diagnosis I hated so much, I started asking questions to the one who made me. God spoke and said, 'Aimee, I love you, and pills don't define you. I define you.' For the first time in my life, I believed it."

Since the great Fall in the Garden of Eden, humanity has struggled with mental illness. From Cain's impulsive murder of his brother Abel (Gen. 4:8-10) to the prophet Elijah's fearful cry for God to take his life (1 Kings 19:4) to King David's sleepless nights spent groaning and weeping (Psalm 6:6-7) to Mary Magdalene's demonic stronghold (Luke 8:2), the Bible is full of examples of those who exhibited various types of psychological disorders. And, while the Lord allows such illnesses to still exist, there is no person so far gone that He cannot reach. Whether through miraculous healing or prescribed medicines, the counseling of the Holy Spirit or a licensed professional here on earth, the Lord's power can manifest itself in many ways to bring healing to your mind.

Because God created all of you (body, mind, soul, and spirit), He wants every area of your life to be well and whole. He recognizes that when one area is sick, the others can be affected as well, and He knows your thoughts carry power because He created you that way. That's why He provides so many verses in Scripture to encourage you in where to set your thoughts (Phil. 4:8; Col. 3:2; Isaiah 26:3, to name a few). These verses can give you hope when there doesn't seem to be very much.

Now, the enemy of your soul will try to convince you that there is no hope when one of these areas of your life is failing.

But he is especially crafty when it comes to the area of your mind. After all, he is the father of lies (John 8:44), and creating chaos and confusion in your mind is his specialty. Cunningly, he will use whatever means he can to do that. Past trauma and shame. Present joys and gifts. Future fears and worries. The enemy will take them all and twist them into a ball of delusional thoughts, leaving you to desperately try to unscramble the lies.

Nearly 2000 years ago, the Apostle Paul could see the schemes of the enemy, and he all but begs you to have a battle plan. Paul literally pleads with you to demolish every argument that sets itself up against the knowledge of God and take every thought captive to Christ (2 Cor.10:5). The original Greek meaning of the word *captive* meant to make it a "subservient prisoner." You are to bind that negative, delusional thought and prepare it to be submissive to Jesus' ways and His Word. Keep in mind, sometimes you are the lone officer who takes that prisoner captive, and sometimes you need to call in the reinforcements.

Just like you see a doctor when your body is sick, there are moments when medical help is needed in order for you to achieve mental health. There is no shame in asking for help and receiving support from someone who will point you down the path of a clear mind. So, today, assess your thoughts. Are they holding up to God's Word and who He says you are? Or are you struggling to take that thought captive and need support? Lean into God today. Find help if needed. Know you aren't alone. There is hope. Trust in the Lord's unfailing love.

As Aimee began accepting her mental illness instead of fighting it, the Lord led her to start writing and speaking about her disease.

"As I wrote about my illness, the shame I felt began to slowly slip away," Aimee said. She learned to laugh again and began to think of herself with grace and love. Mental illness didn't define her anymore. "I'm defined by who He says I am, and I can live my purpose through relationship, dependence, and trust in Him. I hope through my story you will see that God does turn beauty from ashes. Daily, we need to give Him our hard things, and I promise He will grow gardens. If you are in the midst of a mental health struggle or have a family member, do not be afraid. God may or may not give you complete physical healing on this side of Heaven, but I promise He is in the business of healing your heart and soul, and that is worth it."

A Closing Prayer

Lord, I claim every area of my life for your honor and glory: body, mind, soul, and spirit. I praise you for giving me a sound mind, and I pray you will keep it in perfect peace. When delusional thoughts sneak in, help me refocus my thoughts back on you. Rewire the toxicity in my thoughts to thankfulness and renew my mind. Thank you for giving me the Holy Spirit as my Counselor. I ask you to help me always seek His guidance. Amen.

To listen to Aimee's story, go to www.storytellerslive.org /wherehopemeetsyou and look for "Hope in Mental Illness."

Day 20

Hope in Fear

"For I, the LORD your God, hold your right hand;
it is I who say to you, 'Fear not,
I am the one who helps you.'"
—Isaiah 41:13

In her young adult years, Julie would have characterized herself as fearless. "I never knew fear, and I was never scared." Then, years later, two incredibly frightening instances in her life shook her world, and that shaking invited fear to move in for the next eight years. The first took place on a Sunday, as Julie came home from running errands. "I see a stranger in my kitchen with a gun to my baby girl's head." While Julie's fearlessness took over that day and the gunman was caught, she said, "That night, he stole a lot more from my family than just my valuables. He stole my peace. He stole my security. I never got out of the fight or flight response." This fear weighed heavily on Julie, especially when it came to her family. "I refused to lay them at God's feet. I thought I could protect them better than God." Then, years later, a second incident brought Julie's fight with fear full circle as her husband, who had never been sick, was suddenly in complete heart failure. "I was weary. I was exhausted, and I truly wanted to give up." But the Lord had different plans for Julie. He would use this health crisis to bring her freedom as He began revealing her mistrust of Him and how her family had become an idol in her life. "I could feel the Lord's presence working on me. He so desperately wanted to free me, but only I could be the one to let go. All He wanted was for me to say, 'You are all I need.'" Julie finally relinquished her fears and control to God, as she said, "'OK, Lord, I give up. You love them more than I do. And they're safe with you.' And at that moment, declaring those words out loud, every single chain broke. I physically felt it. I was free."

Fear can come like a thief in the night, unexpectedly robbing you of peace, joy, and contentment. In its wake, you are left with an imagination that runs wild, a body that cannot rest, and a controlling spirit that works overtime to prepare you for a battle that hasn't yet taken place (and most likely never will). There is no doubt, fear is a destructive force that can paralyze you, isolate you, and relentlessly torment you. And, if that wasn't enough, fear constantly clamors for your attention. You must fight it with the shield of faith and silence it with the mouthpiece of God's sovereignty.

Scripture tells us again and again that we are in a spiritual war, and because of that, the weapons we fight with are not the weapons of the world. This is why the apostle Paul tells us to "take up the shield of faith, with which you can extinguish all the flaming darts of the evil one." (Eph. 6:16). When Paul wrote this to the church in Ephesus, he no doubt brought the imagery of Roman soldiers to the minds of his readers. Those soldiers, when in battle, would dip the tips of their arrows into flammable material and set them on fire. Then, the arrows, when fired, had the capability of burning their victim to death or even destroying a city. Paul emphatically said the shield of faith can extinguish the arrows of the evil one, rendering them powerless. Every fiery dart of fear Satan sends your way can be extinguished when it collides with your faith. You must pick up your shield every minute of every day, as those arrows can attack abruptly!

If faith is your shield, the certainty of God's sovereignty is your silencer. Fear cannot have the last word when it is sifted through the supremacy of your Father. Knowing God is in control means there is no suffering, no affliction, and no circumstance in your life that is random. Everything that happens to you can be used to bring good into your life, sanctification to your soul, and strength to your shield of faith. You find peace in knowing your life and the lives of those you love are in the hands of a compassionate God, a God who calls your heart to not be troubled or afraid (John 14:27). It is in the realm of God's sovereignty where you will discover your confidence and your courage. It is where you can begin quieting your fearful thoughts, calming your concerns, and worshipping your worries away.

The phrases "do not fear" or "do not be afraid" occur over a hundred times in God's Word. This is not happenstance. Let the repetition serve as a reminder that God understands your fears are inevitable on this side of Heaven, and that He also wants you to find comfort in knowing He is in control. He wants you to know that He will take hold of your right hand. He will help you (Isaiah 41:13). And, because of those promises, fear is not victorious; the Lord is. And, as His child, you are as well. So, grab your shield of faith, hold onto your silencer of sovereignty, and rest in the knowledge that the Lord is your refuge and your strength (Psalm 46:1).

After Julie gave control of her life and those she loves over to God, she said the next few months were the sweetest in her life. "God did so much for me," Julie recalled. "He did way more than I asked or could even imagine. He truly led me to those green pastures, and I found rest." Julie's husband's health was completely restored, and it was a miracle her husband says was used to save and free Julie from her fears. "I walked through some valleys and didn't let my shepherd lead me. These days, I enjoy walking with my shepherd, knowing that if I fall back or if I wander off, He'll leave the 99 and come back for me," Julie said. "There are many things that chain us. Fear just happened to be mine. Let the Lord carry you because He longs to carry His children. And He is the good, good shepherd."

A Closing Prayer

Father, you know each one of my fears and the source from which they stem. Help me to lay each of them at your feet. Remind me every day to pick up my shield of faith and trust completely in your sovereignty. You are my good shepherd who longs to lead me beside quiet waters and restore my soul (Psalm 23:2-3). Help me follow your path of peace instead of letting my fears lead me. Amen.

To listen to Julie's story, go to www.storytellerslive.org/wherehopemeetsyou and look for "Hope in Fear."

Day 21

Hope in Shame

"Fear not, for you will not be ashamed;
be not confounded, for you will not be disgraced;
for you will forget the shame of your youth, and the reproach
of your widowhood you will remember no more."
—Isaiah 54:4

Chapple was a strong-willed, middle child who put a lot of pressure on herself to be perfect all the time. "When I would make a mistake, I would get so down on myself because I felt like such a disappointment," Chapple reflected. "And there is a theme in my life of just feeling like I'm not good enough." As Chapple started her junior year of high school, she began down a path of alcohol and boys to shake off her insecurities. It was a path that led her to an unplanned pregnancy in college. "I really thought that I had screwed up my life. I thought that I was never going to recover. I thought that no one would ever want me because no man would ever want someone who had messed up their life like that and ended up a single mom."

For Chapple, a marriage that ended in divorce a year later only left her more devastated and broken. And while, by the grace of

God, she graduated from college, she found herself drowning in shame. Chapple and her daughter moved back home, and, at her mother's prompting, she attended a church service that would turn out to be directly ordained by God.

In the sermon, the pastor spoke about how God can take an old creation and make it into something brand new. The words hit home in Chapple's heart. "I cannot tell you the feelings of shame and worthlessness I felt at that time in my life. I just never thought I would be able to please the Lord, my family, anybody. And the Lord met me in that moment. I'm going to make you brand new. And I surrendered."

Poor choices. Bad decisions. Agonizing regrets. These are the building blocks of shame. Sometimes those blocks are placed in your life by your own doing, and sometimes by the actions of someone else. Regardless, they can quickly create seemingly impenetrable walls around your heart and mind; walls of shame that wreak havoc on you emotionally, mentally, and especially spiritually. Walls that feel impossible to tear down. However, there is hope in the midst of shame, and it's found in a beautiful, comforting chapter from the Old Testament book of Isaiah.

Isaiah 54 was written during the Babylonian captivity of the nation of Israel. God's chosen people had been exiled from their native land and were living in a culture very different from what God had planned for them. It was a time of deep regret and disgrace for the people as they reflected on past choices. In this chapter, God brings His people hope as He promises them future redemption. He tells them He will bring restoration after their exile. He will replace their shame with a fruitful future. He will completely remove their humiliation and disgrace. In this glorious chapter, God's unwavering love, mercy, and kindness are repeatedly spoken of, giving God's people the encouragement they needed to look toward their future with confident hope and the expectation that His blessing and favor still rested on them. They were not defined by, or left in, their past mistakes.

Like the people held in captivity in Babylon, you and I can easily hold onto the shame and regrets of our past, leaving us spiritually paralyzed in our relationship with the Lord and in the work He would have us do. This is why the Apostle Paul tells us to forget what is behind (our failures and disappointments as well as our accomplishments and achievements) and strain toward what is ahead (Phil. 3:13). The phrase "forget what is behind" means you no longer care for those particular things, and you purposely neglect thinking about them. You don't necessarily forget that they happened, but you stop dwelling on them or finding your identity in them. Instead, you "press on toward the goal for the prize of the upward call of God in Christ Jesus" (Phil. 3:14). The Lord wants you to see yourself as a new creation as a child of God; the old has passed away, and the new has come (2 Cor. 5:17). Shame and disgrace are removed. Grace and acceptance are established.

Today, allow the Lord's love, mercy, and kindness to become wrecking balls for the walls of shame and guilt you have constructed within your life. Believe and receive God's promises and rest in the confident hope He gives you to forget the disgrace of your past. And begin building on the solid foundation of who Jesus Christ says you are forgiven, free, and made brand new!

After that moment of surrender, life as a single mother remained hard for Chapple, but God began doing a great work within her. Through prayer, Bible study, and even dreams, the Lord began healing her shame-filled heart and replacing it with His love and His truths. "He saw all of my mistakes, and He saw all my troubles, and He still chose to die for me," Chapple said of her Heavenly Father. "That's love. That's real love. And I got broken free from so much shame."

Chapple eventually remarried, had two more children, created a successful business, and God continued to redeem her story. She can now look back on her life, even in the messy and the hard, and see God's love for her. Isaiah 61:7 has been a verse she has claimed over her life. "It says, instead of your shame, you will receive a double portion. And instead of dishonor, they will rejoice in their lot. And I am just so thankful. I'm grateful that God freed me from shame. He has given me a new life. I know that without the suffering, I would not know how beautiful God really is. I'm so grateful to have walked through what I have to get to the other side."

A Closing Prayer

Lord, thank you for your promise to make me brand new and for the power you give me to break free from the bondage of shame. Thank you for removing the shame of my past and leading me into a fruitful future. Help me to accept this gift from you and to let go of my regrets so that I may live the life you have intended for me to live here on this earth - bringing all glory and honor to you. Amen.

To listen to Chapple's story, go to www.storytellerslive.org /wherehopemeetsyou and look for "Hope in Shame."

Day 22

Hope in Waiting

"Our soul waits for the LORD; he is our help and our shield.
For our heart is glad in him, because we trust
in his holy name. Let your steadfast love, O LORD,
be upon us, even as we hope in you."
—Psalm 33:20–22

In Amber's twenties and thirties, the Lord began writing unwanted storylines of waiting into her life. The first came soon after college graduation, while Amber stood by and watched friend after friend get married. This difficult season began a line of thinking that something was lacking within her. "I never went to Scripture to check that because it was so real to me. It became a truth in my head," Amber reflected, "and that became my narrative for a long time. It's like I was waiting on the Lord to do something, but not pursuing that He would at the same time."

As Amber waited, the Lord began to work in her heart, revealing to her that He had a purpose for her life. So, she chose to start walking in His truths and embracing her waiting. And, at the age of 36, she got married. But, soon after the wedding, a new storyline of waiting began to be written as she traveled the long and exhausting road of infertility.

Month after month, Amber and her husband waited, prayed, and trusted. Finally, after choosing to undergo IVF treatments and recruiting everyone she knew to pray, Amber found out she was pregnant! Her waiting was over. Or was it? During the 25th week of her pregnancy, Amber's body began to go into labor. And this ushered in Amber's most strenuous season of waiting yet.

Who hasn't been in the "in between"? That space of time where you are waiting. From minor waitings, like waiting to see if you made the team, to major waitings, like waiting for a diagnosis, the "in between" can be unsettling to say the least. And, when the "in between" lands in your prayer life, waiting for God to answer can be one of the most restless and discouraging seasons of your spiritual journey.

Let's face it, the Lord's timing rarely matches ours. We want our prayers to be answered precisely when we think they should be. But that's not how God works. He wants you to get closer to Him in the "in between." To embrace the "in between." Because, when embraced, He knows this prayer-filled waiting period can deepen your love and hope in Him more than any other spiritual discipline.

There are many examples of waiting in the Bible—some good, some great, and some not so good. You have Abraham and Sarah, who played the waiting game pretty well, until Sarah took matters into her own hands and gave her maidservant, Hagar, to Abraham so he could sleep with her. Sarah's mistrust of God's timing didn't thwart His promise of a son, but it did create havoc in her life,

Abraham's, Hagar's, and, quite honestly, the lives of the future nation of Israel (Gen. 16).

There is Joseph, who, after being sold into slavery by his own brothers, gives a flawless example to follow in seasons of waiting. Joseph was mistreated, falsely accused, betrayed, and endured years of unjust imprisonment, yet he remained faithful in trusting God throughout it all. In the end, Joseph found himself second in command over the entire empire and in a position to save countless lives, including his own family (Gen. 37-50).

Then, in the book of Exodus, on the other end of the waiting spectrum, you have the Israelites who, after they escaped from slavery in Egypt, demonstrated a failure to wait for God on numerous occasions. Their refusal to wait well landed an entire generation dying in the wilderness, never to see the Promised Land. These are just three examples from a Bible filled with countless other stories on waiting.

In addition, repeatedly in the Psalms, you read about the importance of waiting and how it plays a role in your spiritual growth. You wait looking for God to be your help and shield (Psalm 33:20). You wait, knowing His Word will be your guide (Psalm 130:5). You wait confidently, resting in the fact that He sees you in the stillness (Psalm 37:7). This word "wait" in Hebrew means to have expectant hope. You know God is going to come through for you. And, you know His goodness is on the other side. In the challenging season of the "in between," you rest in the knowledge that God is enough. And, because He is enough, you wait in anticipation of His perfect plan of rescue (Lam. 3:24-26)

Training yourself to wait well doesn't come naturally. It involves earnestly and actively practicing your faith. It involves surrendering control of your life, intently seeking God's plan for your life, and patiently trusting the Holy Spirit to guide you throughout the process. It's not easy, but the result is worth it. So, today, watch in hope for the Lord and wait for your Savior. He will hear you (Micah 7:7).

When Amber's body began to go into labor, her emotions took over, and she started to panic. "The only prayer I knew to pray was 'calm me down.' And so, I just kept saying that." As Amber prayed, she began recalling God's character. "In that moment, I felt the Holy Spirit say, 'Here's what we're going to cling to: We know God is good. We know God is in control. And we know God never leaves us.' And so, I kept saying those things over and over again."

By God's grace, Amber didn't go into full-blown labor that day, but she was admitted into the hospital and put on bed rest. And, after three weeks of resting and waiting, Amber finally delivered. But her waiting still wasn't over. While she left the hospital, the baby had to stay in the NICU. It would be two more months of wearisome waiting before he could come home. They were months filled with reading her Bible, praying, and trusting in the Lord's plan.

Reflecting on the Lord's timing, Amber can now see how her many difficult waiting seasons brought her to new levels of confident hope and unwavering trust she would never have known. After all, she said, "If you never had to trust Him, you would never say He's trustworthy."

A Closing Prayer

Lord, you know how difficult it is to wait for something I want so badly to come true in my life. You know my dreams and desires.

Help me to surrender those dreams and desires to you and increase my faith and trust in who you are. I believe you are enough for me in my seasons of waiting. I will wait for you, Lord, and put my trust in you (Isaiah 8:7). Amen.

To listen to Amber's story, go to www.storytellerslive.org/wherehopemeetsyou and look for "Hope in Waiting."

Day 23

Hope in God's Word

"For whatever was written in former days was written for our instruction, that through endurance and through the encouragement of the Scriptures we might have hope."
—Romans 15:4

"The Lord chose me prior to even being in my mom's womb," Rekeshia began as she considered her story. At a young age, the Word of God was planted in her heart due to years of Vacation Bible School. It was a blessing that Rekeshia could see its significance, as the Lord knew she would need His foundational truths in her future.

As she got older, Rekeshia married her high school sweetheart, Cleo, and just a year later, she found out she was pregnant. However, the road of pregnancy proved to be difficult for Rekeshia as she suffered through two miscarriages. "It was not a time for our faith to turn on God because of our losses. We decided to continue to rest in His care."

Over the years, Rekeshia and Cleo held onto the Lord and trusted His Word. Eventually, they were blessed with the birth of two girls. And life was great. Until the most devastating day of

Rekeshia's life came: Cleo was killed in an automobile accident. Instantly, Rekeshia was a single mom. She was 33 years old, with a two-year-old and a seven-year-old. "It changed my life forever. It changed my perspective forever. It changed my urgency forever. It changed my heart forever. It changed my household forever." Rekeshia knew her only hope was to find comfort in the Lord's presence and in His Word as she processed her extreme grief. "At an early age, I was taught far greater is He who is in me than he who is in the world," Rekeshia recalled. "I can do all things through Christ who strengthens me," became her heart's cry.

The Word of God is powerful. It is alive and active. It gives the weary confidence and comfort. It gives courage and perseverance to the weak. It is a counselor, a teacher, and a friend. And, when allowed, it is a spiritual heart surgeon, laying open your heart, discerning your spiritual health, and working to strengthen and heal you in supernatural ways.

God's Word isn't just a collection of stories; it is a continual source of life. But, do you see it that way? Is it your "go to" when things don't go quite as planned? Is it your stability in the storms of suffering? Is it your protection when fears emerge? For most of us, the answer is rarely a resounding "yes," and because of that, we miss out on the authority God's Word carries. We must recognize the power within our reach and learn to grasp for His Word and His promises within its pages.

Countless verses emphasize the importance of reading and hearing God's Word. It is a lamp to your feet and a light to your path (Psalm 119:105). It teaches, rebukes, corrects, and trains you for righteousness (2 Tim. 3:16). It is a flowing stream of water providing nourishment to your soul (Psalm 1:2-3). It is the sword for which you fight off the lies of the enemy (Eph. 6:17). It is how you know Jesus and find freedom in Christ (John 8:31-32). It is the tool used to sanctify you, making you more into the image of Christ (John 17:17). And everything written within its pages is there to give you endurance, encouragement, and hope (Romans 15:4). No wonder the author of Psalm 119 says five times, "I have put my hope in your word."

When you put your hope in God's Word, you wholeheartedly trust and believe it. You actively hold onto the promises and character of God, knowing, without a doubt, He will be faithful, especially when the circumstances of life become overwhelming. You recognize when you are in situations where you are believing "in" God versus believing God (there is a huge difference)! And, most importantly, you don't act from your feelings, as they can mislead you. You choose to act from your faith. You choose to shift your thoughts to God. You choose to place your confidence in His Word. You choose to expect Him to provide your needs. You choose to rely on His knowledge for what is best in your life. You choose Him to guide you and teach you because your hope is in Him all day long (Psalm 25:5).

If you have been searching for answers in your life, go to God's Word. If you have been needing comfort and encouragement, go to God's Word. If you have been longing for a partner, an advocate, or a confidant, go to God's Word. It will never disappoint you. It will always give answers. It will forever bring hope.

After Cleo passed away, Rekeshia's knowledge of God's Word went from reciting it to realizing it is true. "I thank God for the

Word," she said. Romans 15:13 was a verse she clung to: "May the God of hope fill you with all joy and peace in believing, so that by the power of the Holy Spirit you may abound in hope." "Loss is not lost. There is hope even in the midst of despair. There is peace even in the midst of chaos," Rekeshia said. "It's all about perspective and belief and faith."

As the years passed, Rekeshia shifted her thoughts and began counting her blessings, and that shift proved life-changing for her. "He will keep you in perfect peace. I believe that. I have had to keep my mind on Him. And, since I believe the Word of God, my life experiences have shifted me from believing to actually living it. The Lord cares. He remains present. I'm a believer. I believed all of my life. I won't stop believing. He's brought me too far to leave me. And so I'm thankful that the Lord has my best interests at heart."

A Closing Prayer

Lord, thanking you for your Word just doesn't seem like enough. It is my lifeline, my everything. When life becomes difficult, direct me to what you say in its pages. Open my eyes that I may see wonderful things in your Holy Scripture, and help me live out your truths, believing your promises in every aspect of my life. Amen.

To listen to Rekeshia's story, go to www.storytellerslive.org/wherehopemeetsyou and look for "Hope in God's Word."

Day 24

Hope in God's Provision

"As for the rich in this present age, charge them not to be haughty, nor to set their hopes on the uncertainty of riches, but on God, who richly provides us with everything to enjoy."
—1 Timothy 6:17

The first time Kristen recognized the Lord's provision came soon after she married. She and her husband found themselves in a new city, with new jobs (that paid little to nothing), and a baby on the way. "It was one of those things where we can't buy our own food, how are we going to buy diapers for a baby. And the Lord continued to provide. There were so many people that just showed up for us, provisions that you don't even know are a provision at the time."

Looking back, Kristen can clearly see how the Lord showed up, but at the time, comparison with others settled in her soul. And, on top of that, a season of medical needs for her baby arose, leaving Kristen questioning God and His ways. "Why are you allowing us to continue to go through these seasons?" Kristen would ask. "And what I couldn't see then was that He was really preparing us for a future season that we had no idea was coming."

Western culture makes it so easy to put our hope in the things of this world, with money being at the top of the list. Financial security screams at us from all directions: build an emergency fund, contribute to your 401(k), save for retirement, diversify your investments, purchase insurance to protect your assets, and the list goes on and on. And while these are all legitimate and worthy of your attention, financial security remains uncertain. The only constant in this world worthy of your hope is looking to God alone as your provider, the ultimate source of your provision (1 Tim. 6:17).

Jehovah Jireh is one of the many different names of God found in the Old Testament. The name means "The Lord will provide," and a pretty dramatic story in Genesis chapter 22 introduces us to it. The story begins with a disturbing, strange command from God: to offer his promised son, Isaac, as a burnt offering. You watch as Abraham shows insurmountable faith and trust in God as he obediently begins to carry out the assignment. Then, dramatically, at the last minute, you see the Lord provide another offering in Isaac's place. After this sensational set of events, Abraham then names the mountain where he was called to make the sacrifice "Jehovah Jireh" because of God's gracious provision of a substitute.

This story is more than just a breathtaking illustration of faith and obedience. It really is a picture of God's grace, His continual provision, and His all-encompassing wisdom. Notice, Jehovah Jireh is not "The LORD *did* provide," but "The LORD *will* provide." In other words, the name doesn't refer to just past events; the name anticipates God's ongoing future provision in your life as well. In Genesis 22, Jehovah Jireh provided a sacrifice to save Isaac. However, that provision, given thousands of years ago, also foreshadowed God sending His Son, Jesus Christ, as a sacrifice for you.

Jesus was sacrificed to not only save you, but to give you an abundant life as well (John 10:10). There's no need too small He doesn't know about and no need too big He can't provide for you. Philippians 4:19 says, "And my God will supply every need of yours according to his riches in glory in Christ Jesus." God wants to meet your every need in Jesus, but you must read this in the context of the whole Bible. Matthew 6:33 says, "But seek first the kingdom of God and his righteousness, and all these things will be added to you." That word *seek* means "to aim or strive for." You are to wholeheartedly strive for God's kingdom and His righteousness, and then these things will be given to you. Your relationship with God needs to be your number one priority because everything you need is found in Him. Do you believe that? Everything you need is found in God!

When you seek God's face and His presence more than you seek His hand and what He can do for you, you find your needs, wants, and desires change. Your mind and heart become set on what God's best is for you. The challenge is to fully trust in God as Jehovah Jireh. Trust Him to meet your needs today. Trust Him to be your provider for healing, comfort, wisdom, peace, and joy. Live confidently in His grace, forgiveness, mercy, and strength. And rest in the confident hope of knowing God is your Jehovah Jireh.

As the years went by, Kristen's family grew. She and her husband continued to see the Lord providing for them in miraculous ways. But then, beginning in December of 2020, her family encountered several difficult life circumstances and attacks from the enemy, a season that lasted over 18 months. It left Kristen doubting God's provision once again. "I knew that God was Provider, but I also had very raw human emotions. I know that you will provide this, whatever it might be, but I would also beg Him to end the season of trial." In an effort not to be a burden, Kristen began downplaying her situation to others and to herself. She felt safer being independent rather than dependent on God and others. But soon, it became clear to her that her inability to be vulnerable really stemmed from her pride, her fear, and her unbelief that God would come through as a provider for her. It was a lie that brought her to a deep desire to know God more. And the Lord, in His perfect plan of provision, met Kristen and her husband right where they were. "It created a shift in our depth and in our posture. It created a shift in our dependency on Him and less on ourselves," Kristen gratefully reflected. And, while it's still a daily surrender for her, Kristen now rests in the knowledge that God knows exactly what she needs. "Whether I allow Him to or I don't, He's going to provide. But I want to be on the ride with Him. I want to be dependent on Him, and I want my safety to come from Him and not from my independence or from myself."

A Closing Prayer

Heavenly Father, I praise you for being my Jehovah Jireh and for your perfect provision in my life. Thank you for caring about my needs and for your promise to meet them. I sit in awe of the provision found in Jesus' sacrifice on the cross, and I ask you to help me recognize that all my needs are found in you alone. Amen.

To listen to Kristen's story, go to www.storytellerslive.org/wherehopemeetsyou and look for "Hope in God's Provision."

Day 25

Hope in God's Sovereignty

"Yours, O LORD, is the greatness and the power and the glory and the victory and the majesty, for all that is in the heavens and in the earth is yours. Yours is the kingdom, O LORD, and you are exalted as head above all."
—1 Chronicles 29:11

When Susan got married, she had a definite plan for her life. "I was going to have four girls. We were going to do hair and ballet, and they were going to love school and be very into academics. None of those things happened. We ended up with five boys," Susan joked. "And I would often think, Lord, you got this all wrong."

While Susan can laugh about her thwarted plans, seriousness settles in her soul as she begins to reflect on the season the Lord taught her the importance of resting in His will and His sovereignty over her life. "Four of those children we raised through adulthood. Russell was the child we lost shortly after birth," Susan reflected. "It was just the most devastating thing I had ever faced. I was so angry with God." Susan thought if the Lord cared for her, He would never have allowed it to happen, so she decided she didn't want anything to do with God. However, deep in her heart, Susan knew the Scriptures were the only place she would find answers.

Reluctantly, Susan dug into the book of Job. "Job wanted to know why he had lost everything, and God didn't answer his questions," Susan discovered. "What He did do for Job was He showed him who was in charge. He showed him that He was sovereign." This concept of God's sovereignty began resonating with Susan and ultimately helped her realize her need to let go of control and trust the Lord. "His ways were higher than my ways and His thoughts higher than my thoughts. He saw the whole picture, and I didn't. So, I chose to submit and to accept what He had shown me. He didn't give me the answer I wanted because He was the answer."

Embracing the sovereignty of God is foundational to thriving in the faith-filled Christian life, trusting His ways, His timing, and His will. On paper, it seems simple enough. In reality, it is much more difficult. We long to understand the "whys" behind the circumstances and events surrounding our lives. We crave contentment and peace in the chaos, confidence and clarity in the uncertainty, comfort and happiness in the pain. And so, we work hard to satisfy those desires by organizing, planning, and controlling the narratives of our stories. However, when we recognize God as Creator and Owner of it all (Deut. 10:14) and accept His right to do as He pleases with our lives, we find it's in the resting, and the letting go that we find serenity and stability in our journeys.

One of the greatest examples of trusting God's sovereignty is King David in the Old Testament. David's complete submission to God's authority is first seen when he was running for his life from King Saul. Repeatedly, you read of David crying out to the Lord as his vindicator, his refuge, and his rescuer. David was determined to keep his heart steadfast in the Lord, praising Him for His unfailing love and proclaiming His omnipotent power in the Heavens and on earth (Psalm 57). David shows us, in times of turmoil, that resting in God's sovereignty begins by magnifying His name.

In moments of extreme sorrow and pain, David also recognized the Lord's authority to do with his life whatever He pleased. This is seen after his affair with Bathsheba as the prophet Nathan tells David the calamity he is about to face, including the death of his infant son. David pleaded with the Lord for the child's life. However, when the baby died, David stopped grieving, went to the house of the Lord to worship, and then comforted his wife (2 Sam. 12). David shows us, amid anguish and grief, that worship brings recognition of God's sovereignty and strength to a weary heart.

Finally, David's story gives us a glimpse into his humility when it came to God's purpose for his life. After the Ark of the Covenant was brought to Jerusalem, David was determined to build a great temple to house the Ark. However, God rejected David as the builder saying, "You have shed much blood and have waged great wars. You shall not build a house to my name, because you have shed so much blood before me on the earth." (1 Chron. 22:8). The Lord went on to say that David's son, Solomon, would build it instead. Without question or discontentment, David humbly accepted the Lord's decision. And as he passed the assignment to Solomon, David offered this beautiful prayer, recognizing the Lord's sovereignty once again. "Yours, Lord, is the greatness and the power and the glory and the majesty and the splendor, for everything in heaven and earth is yours. Yours, Lord is the kingdom; you are exalted as head over all . . . You are the ruler of all things . . . everything comes from you, and we have given you only what comes from your hand . . . All of it belongs to you" (1 Chron. 29:11-16). It's a prayer we can all remember in times of questioning the Lord's will for our lives.

So, today, emulate King David and embrace God's sovereignty over your own story. Magnify His name. Worship His Majesty. Sit humbly in His presence. Rest in knowing God reigns over *all* creation and *all* people to bring His perfect will in *all* things.

Susan's revelation of God's sovereignty was one she would fiercely cling to over the years, as there were many more moments of tragedy and loss. As her boys got older, there was the discovery of one of her boys being sexually abused as a child. Then, two of her other sons struggled on and off with drug addictions. And, tragically, one of those sons, at the age of 32, died from a heroin overdose. "It was a devastating time for our whole family, but we know that he is with the Lord," Susan said. "I think about all these things and what the Lord has taught me throughout all of this. And most of all, He has taught me that He is sovereign over all things. There is nothing that touches my life that He does not allow to touch my life. And, therefore, I don't fear the future because I know He is in control."

A Closing Prayer

Lord, thank you for your sovereignty. Today, I recognize that all creation is yours to do as you please. Give me strength in the hard moments, purpose in the painful moments, and joy in the moments of sorrow. And thank you for working all things for my good (Rom. 8:28). Amen.

To listen to Susan's story, go to www.storytellerslive.org/where hopemeetsyou and look for "Hope in God's Sovereignty."

Day 26

Hope in God's Grace

"For by grace you have been saved through faith.
And this is not your own doing; it is the gift of God,
not a result of works, so that no one may boast."
—Ephesians 2:8–9

Rachel was the peacemaker, perfectionist, and pleaser in her seemingly picture-perfect family. However, as is often the case, pictures aren't reality. Rachel also grew up under the pressures of having a mother who struggled with alcoholism and a father who was an enabler, leaving her succumbing to the role of caretaker. It was a role that led her to believe the lie that if she did all the right things for God, life would be easier. "I developed a theological understanding that I could earn God's favor by being good enough," Rachel said. "And, if I had His favor, then He would owe me. And while my family was falling apart, I was a good Christian, and I wasn't going to let it break me. And then, one day, the Lord would reward me for that."

Rachel's misunderstanding of the gospel led her down a path of comparison, insecurity, and spiritual depression. Until, one day, the Lord met her and asked, "Will you be defined by your victimhood or by my grace?" It was a question that changed the trajectory of Rachel's life. "In that moment, I did business with the Lord, and I stepped into the belief that He could heal me and change my critical spirit, and set me free from my fear, my insecurities, and my striving to make myself good enough. And I learned at this point that my woundedness, if left undealt with, would lead me to the exact same place as undealt sin. I needed the Lord to intervene and heal me."

We live in a society where we are constantly trying to be good enough. Good enough to make the team. Good enough to get the job. Good enough to win the award. Good enough to be accepted, valued, and loved. And while self-effort and putting your best foot forward aren't bad ideas, when you base your worth on them, you will inevitably find yourself in a place of exhaustion, frustration, and depression. The reason why? You were never created to live a life centered around striving to be "good enough." You were created to live a life centered around surrendering to God and His grace.

The gift of grace, found through the sacrifice of Jesus Christ on the cross, is undeniably God's greatest act of kindness and mercy to mankind. It redeems your past, reshapes your present, and redirects your future. It saves you (Acts 15:11), justifies you (Rom. 3:24), and sanctifies you (Titus 2:11-13). It gives you access to the throne room of God, where you can find continuous comfort, strength, healing, and transformation (Heb. 4:16; 13:9). Grace is never interrupted. Never limited. Never depleted. This is the hope found in Jesus (John 1:14;16), and it is freely given to everyone who will accept it (Eph. 1:6).

However, for most of us, accepting a "free" gift seems contrary to our cultural norms. We think there have to be strings attached. We think we owe the giver something in return. We feel obligated to try to reciprocate the gift in some way. So we begin working to feel worthy of the gift. We overextend ourselves. We overexert ourselves. We exhaust ourselves. And ultimately, this can lead to a strained, bitter, and unpleasant relationship with the giver. Unfortunately, this is the predicament many followers of Christ find themselves in due to their misunderstanding of God's grace.

Grace is not based on what you have done, what you are doing, or what you will do. If it were, grace would no longer be grace (Rom. 11:6), and people could boast (Eph. 2:8-9). Grace is God's unmerited favor. It is the result of a loving, pursuing, generous Father whose greatest desire is for His children to live under His covering. And when a child of God humbly accepts His covering, a position of gratitude begins to emerge. This position instills a longing to live for Christ, not from a works-based mindset, but from a mindset of gratefulness. You acknowledge the grace given to you, and you mindfully want to live a holy life (2 Tim. 1:9), not out of obligation, but out of love to the Father who has given the gift. Your works are not about what you are doing for the Father, but rather, what the Father is doing in you.

Take a moment to reflect on how you view God's grace. Have you humbly accepted His free gift? If so, are you striving to be worthy of it or resting in knowing you are worthy of it because of Jesus? Are you taking His gift in vain, or are you allowing it to do a work inside of you? Today, thank God for His incredible gift of grace that brings salvation and transformation to your soul!

After Rachel's revelation of the gospel of grace, the next few years were a slow process of growing in that grace and mercy towards herself and others. She began to learn that God's goal with her righteousness wasn't based on her outward appearance of holiness by avoiding sinful behavior and doing good works, but instead on an inward righteousness because of His grace and mercy alone.

Rachel admits that, over the years, it's been a challenge not to revert to her former way of thinking, especially when she began a family of her own. "This was a time in which God revealed to me a lot of things on my inside that needed to be dealt with," Rachel said. "My life, my superficiality, my instinct to control, my desire for the approval of others, and my pride." With gratefulness, Rachel reflects on all the ways in which the Lord has taught her about His unmerited grace, "I look at myself now, and while we're all works in progress until the Lord takes us into eternity, I can see the effects of grace in my life. I lean on the experience and goodness of God to me in spite of myself. And with the belief that God is good, I don't have to be good enough anymore."

A Closing Prayer

Lord, I am so very grateful for your free gift of grace. I am beyond thankful for the strength it gives me in my weaknesses (2 Cor. 12:9-10) and for how it transforms me more into the image of Christ. Help me to always humbly accept your grace and allow it to do its work within me until the day you return to take me home. Amen.

To listen to Rachel's story, go to www.storytellerslive.org/wherehopemeetsyou and look for "Hope in God's Grace."

Day 27

Hope in God's Goodness

"Surely goodness and mercy shall follow me all the days of my life, and I shall dwell in the house of the LORD forever."
—Psalm 23:6

Meghan grew up a self-proclaimed daddy's girl. She was the son he never had. They bonded over many things, but mostly over her love of softball. This sport led her and her family into a personal relationship with the Lord after another softball player invited her to a youth camp. "God had a plan for me the moment that I picked up that ball," Meghan reminisced, "because this girl is going to invite me to this thing at church that really forever changed my life."

Throughout the years that followed, the goodness of God continued to be felt by Meghan as He guided her to the perfect college, then onto the perfect job after college, where she met her future husband. Ultimately, God even led her to the perfect opportunity for her and her husband to move back to her hometown. "God was revealing His goodness through His plan. So, we moved back home closer to family, closer to my parents, and all was well." And all stayed well until one tragedy hit.

One night, while out on a jog, Meghan's father was hit by a car and instantly killed. "Honestly, this was my biggest fear growing up. The man I thought hung the moon, Superman, invincible, was no longer with me." Meghan couldn't breathe. She couldn't move. She confided in a friend that she didn't know if God was still good. Her friend's response led her to the truth she needed to hear. "She grabbed my face, and she said, 'I know God doesn't seem so good right now. I know that this was not part of your plan, but I want you to do this for me. I want you to pick one thing, one thing that you know to be true about His character.'" In that moment, Meghan knew what her "one thing" was: God was good. "I knew over the course of my life, if I had seen anything to be true, it was that He was good and His plan was good."

Have you ever been to the Redwood Forest in California and seen the magnificent giant redwood trees? With trunks close to thirty feet wide, supporting canopy-like branches over 250 feet high, their beauty is something to behold. Underneath the surface of the impressive trunks is a root system that spreads out some 100 feet. The roots intertwine to provide vitality to the trunk, which in turn supports and stabilizes the branches.

When you think of God and the hope found in His goodness, the glorious imagery of these trees comes to mind. God's unconditional love and faithfulness serve as the tree's root system. The enormous, majestic trunk is God's goodness. And the towering, overhanging branches that stem from the trunk are His amazing attributes: His provision, protection, grace, mercy, forgiveness, patience, compassion, peace, and kindness. Goodness is not just what God does. It is who He is.

We see God's goodness as the very being of His essence in the book of Exodus. In this book, God has miraculously led the Israelites out of slavery in Egypt under the leadership of Moses. He has placed them in the wilderness with a promise to lead them back to the land of their ancestors, the Promised Land. However, as we often do, the Israelites had trouble trusting God's goodness in the unfamiliar wilderness, and they reverted to their old ways of living.

God was frustrated with the Israelites to say the least, so frustrated that He debated on allowing His presence to continue with them. In Exodus 33, Moses, desperate for God to remain present, begged to see His glory for the reassurance that he would not be left alone. Faithful to His promise, God obliged Moses' request by saying, ""I will make all my goodness pass before you and will proclaim before you my name 'The LORD.' And I will be gracious to whom I will be gracious, and will show mercy on whom I will show mercy" (Ex. 33:19). God's glory manifested in His goodness.

God could have shown Moses His omnipotent power. He could have shown him His unsurpassed strength. He could have even shown him His righteous anger. But God chose instead to show Moses His goodness. God knew His goodness would give Moses the confidence to trust Him, the courage to keep going, and the faith to endure until the end. God knew Moses needed these things, and He knows you need them too.

Rest assured, God's goodness, as seen in Moses' encounter, is constant and unchanging (James 1:17), and your faith in that goodness should be the same. Faith in God is not transactional. In other words, we can't say "if God is good (in your opinion of good), then I'll have faith." No, faith is relational. You have faith in God because you trust in His goodness as your Father and your Creator.

The familiar words of Psalm 23 end by saying God's goodness and love will follow you all the days of your life (v.6). Do you believe this? Do you know God has been good, He is good, and He will be good? Taste and see that the Lord is good (Psalm 34:8) and discover how He will show you His goodness today.

Days after her father's passing, Meghan began journaling about how she had experienced the Lord's goodness. As she journaled, she saw God's good hands in her life. From spending time with her father and taking pictures of him just days before he passed away to speaking with him twice on the phone the night of the accident, "I truly think God in His goodness was preparing my heart," Meghan said. "None of it took away my sadness and my grief, but it did bring me comfort. It brought me rest. It's like God was showing me all along the way that though my circumstances were not good, He was still good. I have come to believe that if we will trust God in the middle of our pain and our grief or whatever we're walking through, He will show us that sometimes good things and hard things and holy things can all occupy the same space. I know that He is good, so I can trust His plan is good."

A Closing Prayer

Lord, I know you are a good God, but sometimes, when life's circumstances seem overwhelming, it becomes hard for me to rest in your goodness. In these moments, open my eyes to how you have been good to me. Like the majestic redwood trees, help me visualize the branches that spring forth from your "goodness" trunk, covering me with your protection. I trust you, Lord, and I love you. Amen.

To listen to Meghan's story, go to www.storytellerslive.org/wherehopemeetsyou and look for "Hope in God's Goodness."

Day 28

Hope in God's Peace

"May the God of hope fill you with all joy
and peace in believing, so that by the power of the Holy Spirit
you may abound in hope."
—Romans 15:13

It was a beautiful, normal Spring day, and Alesha's job in the pharmaceutical industry had taken her to visit a possible new account. "I love to meet new people, new accounts, and I stepped off the elevator. I mean, the minute I stepped off, I came face to face with a man who had a gun." At first, it didn't register to Alesha that the man had a gun. She had no idea he had just committed a mass shooting. "I just looked at him," Alesha said. "I looked him in the eye. I said hello, and he raised his gun and shot me in the face at point-blank range." In that moment, vivid memories flooded Alesha's mind. She was 48 years old, married, and had three children. Her life passed before her. However, at that moment, she also felt a sense of Heaven. "It was something," Alesha recalled, "It's even hard for me now to put it into words. It was so warm and so peaceful. I had a peace that surrounded me that truly surpassed all understanding."

Alesha didn't feel scared. She didn't feel any pain. She just felt a covering of peace. "I just kept repeating, Jesus, Jesus, Jesus, just over and over again." As Alesha focused her thoughts on Jesus and called on His name, she felt God preserving her life, and as the first responders arrived on the scene, the peace of God continued to be felt. "I remember them holding my hand. But most of all, I remember the peace and the strength that God gave me. I'll never forget that." A few days later, Alesha woke up in the ICU. Loved ones surrounded her, and, once again, calmness settled in her soul. "The Lord had laid this spirit of peace upon me. I really thought I was going to walk out of there. I was going to be OK. The peace that surrounded me was just undeniable. And it was only God."

Life is full of demands and challenges. Relationships come and go. Job opportunities fall apart. Financial struggles hit. A single event can suddenly alter your circumstances, leaving you scrambling to make sense of it all. It's no wonder Jesus warns us that "in the world you will have tribulation" (John 16:33). Troubles are lurking around every corner of life.

However, in the same verse, before His warning, Jesus also says, "I have said these things to you, that in me you may have peace." You *will* have troubles. You *may* have peace. Troubles promised. Peace offered. Jesus is clear: The hope of peace, found in His reassuring presence, is possible amidst your problems and your pain. But notice that it's an offer in exchange for a promise. The ability to experience the benefits of the promise lies within you.

The prophet Isaiah gives two key steps to take toward walking in peace: "You keep him in perfect peace whose mind is stayed on you, because he trusts in you" (Isaiah 26:3). Peace is achieved by first placing your thoughts on God. If you are out of peace, you are most likely out of focus. The word "stayed" in this verse implies a spiritual discipline of leaning into and relying on God. It is intentional, not happenstance, and it is directly related to the second step Isaiah gives for experiencing His peace: trust. As you center your mind on God, the enemies of peace (worry and the need for control) are quieted. You can surrender to God's control, trust His ways, and your soul finds rest.

In his letter to the Philippians, the Apostle Paul also gives two steps to experiencing God's peace. He writes, "Do not be anxious about anything, but in everything by prayer and supplication with thanksgiving let your requests be made known to God. And the peace of God, which surpasses all understanding, will guard your hearts and your minds in Christ Jesus" (Phil. 4:6-7). Recognize the context of the promise Paul gives you here concerning God's supernatural peace. In every situation, pray and petition God for help, but cover those prayers with gratitude. Pray *and* give thanks.

Amid the troubles we encounter, the last thing we usually think about is being grateful for our situation. But that is exactly what Paul tells us to do to experience God's supernatural peace. You take your mind off your flesh (your fear, disappointment, bitterness, and resentment), which leads to death, and you place your mind on the Spirit, which leads to life and peace (Rom. 8:6).

God yearns to give you His peace. He is not stingy with it. In fact, He wants to give you so much peace that you are overflowing with hope by the power of the Holy Spirit (Rom. 15:13). But, He does require that you take steps towards Him for it. Focus on Him. Trust in Him. Pray to Him. Be thankful for Him. These are the stepping stones on the pathway to peace and a stilled soul.

After Alesha woke up in the ICU, she said she was physically destroyed, but because of God's peace, she never felt stronger mentally and spiritually. "That really just kind of stayed with me and carried me through. I mean, that is only God, right? He offered me a peace and a hope and a joy in the most challenging days of my life. And for that, I'm so thankful." Alicia continues to heal to this day, undergoing various medical treatments, and while life is hard, she is back, for the most part, to her normal life.

As she reflects on the day that changed her life forever, she can look back on it with surprising gratitude. "I know that that sounds kind of odd to say with the circumstances that transpired. And I'm only speaking for myself. I cannot speak for the other victims. I know their stories were all different, and I do feel their pain. But what He walked me through in those days brought me a joy and a peace and a really, really acknowledging time in my life. And I don't want to forget that."

A Closing Prayer

Father, thank you for your peace that passes all understanding. When I am walking through difficult circumstances, help me to remain steadfast in my thoughts and trust in you. May I live my life through the power of your Spirit instead of my flesh. And, Lord, help me to live grateful. Grateful for all the many blessings you have bestowed on me through Jesus Christ, as He alone is where true peace is found. Amen.

To listen to Alesha's story, go to www.storytellerslive.org/wherehopemeetsyou and look for "Hope in God's Peace."

Day 29

Hope in God's Pursuing Love

"In this is love, not that we have loved God but that he loved us and sent his Son to be the propitiation for our sins."
—1 John 4:10

Linda was born and raised in Taiwan in a culture that didn't value girls, and as a result, she came to believe she was not valuable. This lie only grew as her home life felt unsafe and insecure, and her blended religion of Taoism and Buddhism left her feeling empty inside. She longed for a family and a faith that was full of love and joy, a desire she carried with her over the years.

As Linda became an adult, through a series of events, she found herself living in Salt Lake City, Utah, and drawn to the Mormon church. Seemingly, it offered Linda everything she wanted, but most importantly, it offered her the idea of an eternal family filled with love, something she craved her entire life. She soon joined the Mormon church, met her husband, and got married.

Linda was on her way to living her dream. However, years later, Linda began to question the Mormon faith she professed. "It was a system that promised peace but only delivered pressure," Linda said. So she began praying for an opportunity to move to a state where she could find freedom, and a job opportunity came up in North Carolina. "We thought God had answered our prayer by providing financial freedom, but how little we knew about His plans and how sovereign and wonderful God is."

Away from her Mormon church home, God began to peel away the false beliefs Linda had accepted as truth. And, in His love, He led her to a desire to discover who He was in the Bible. One night as she cried out to Him, the Lord spoke His love over her. "In that very dark moment, something incredible happened. A Scripture verse came to my mind so clearly. 'I'm the light of the world. Whoever follows me will not walk in darkness, but will have the light of life.' That night changed everything. I chose to put my faith in Jesus Christ alone, not in the religion, not in the organization, but in the living Jesus of the Bible. I realized that He is so much bigger than the Mormon Church. I don't need the church to be safe. I just need Him."

The love of Jesus is relentless. Pursuing you when you question. When you doubt. When you are fearful, faithless, or far away. God's ultimate desire, as a Father cares for His child, is for each soul to know His unconditional, unexplainable love. After all, love is Who God is (1 John 4:8). In fact, your very need for love on this earth is actually a need for God Himself!

Our Father in Heaven operates from an initiating love. In other words, He woos your heart. He pursues you as His perfect bride (John 3:29). You are precious and honored in His sight (Isaiah 43:4). He doesn't love you because of your love for Him

(1 John 4:10). He doesn't love you because of your actions or your worthiness (Rom. 5:8). He simply loves you because He wants you to experience life as His beloved. And He will go to great lengths to help you trust and discover that love.

In Luke 15, Jesus gives three beautiful parables surrounding His pursuing love. The stories are told in response to the religious leaders of the day, the Pharisees, who accused Jesus of spending too much time with sinners. Jesus responds with illustrations about a lost sheep, a lost coin, and a lost son. Through the first two parables, you are given insight into the Lord's heart when it comes to lost souls; the shepherd leaves the 99 to go in search of the one, and it was for one coin the woman scoured her house in search of it. In the final parable, you see the love of God in a different light.

In the parable that most of us know as the Parable of the Prodigal Son, the son is allowed to rebel and leave the love and safety of the Father, but the love of the Father remained steadfast, rejoicing when the son returned home. Jesus' message through all three stories is clear: every person is cherished, valued, and loved by God, and He will always go to great lengths to help every person know their worth and His never-ceasing love.

God wants *you* to rest in His unshakable love. He wants you to know, without a doubt, that His love will never be removed from you (Isaiah 54:10). And He wants you to live your life from the foundation of His love, secure and safe in His arms. Sit with Jesus today and meditate on how He has pursued you over the years. Praise Him for His love that is everlasting and eternal. And then, let the abundance of His love overflow into the lives of those around you.

The day after Linda's revelation from God, she shared her experience with her husband. And quickly after, her husband became the spiritual leader of their family, as his eyes began to open to God's love as well. Their family soon began attending a Christian church and studying the Bible. "It felt incredibly freeing. I met the Jesus of the Bible, the truth, the life. I couldn't go back. I had no desire to return to the lies. It's like when you discover the real, pure living water, you no longer want the fake water. You will know the truth, and the truth will set you free." Linda can now see that when she prayed for God to move them to a different state to find freedom, in His love, He offered her family eternal freedom. "When I finally turned to the Jesus of the Bible, everything began to change. His love isn't manipulative or conditional. It's freeing, healing, and deeply personal. Stepping away from what was never of Him opened the door for me to truly know Him. And, in that freedom, I discovered the peace, hope, and joy that only a real relationship with Jesus Christ can bring."

A Closing Prayer

Father, thank you for your pursuing love. Thank you for searching for me when I am far away and for never leaving me or forsaking me (Heb. 13:5). I praise you for your love that is never ending, a love that saved me and a love that desires to save every soul. Lord, I lift up those who are lost and need you. May your pursuing love engulf them so that they may know the hope to which you have called them. Amen.

To listen to Linda's story, go to www.storytellerslive.org/wherehopemeetsyou and look for "Hope in God's Pursuing Love."

Day 30

Hope in God's Unchanging Faithfulness

"Let us hold fast the confession of our hope
without wavering, for he who promised is faithful."
—Hebrews 10:23

"I always knew I wanted to be a mother to possibly a whole carload of kids," Anna said as she began her story. "When my husband and I decided to start a family, I was pregnant quickly, and I could start to see all of my childhood dreams click into place." Those dreams, however, took an abrupt turn for Anna when her second pregnancy, less than two years later, had life-altering complications and resulted in a miscarriage. "I was devastated, confused, and frankly, I was rip-roaring mad. I was mad at God. I was mad at my body. And I was mad that I had no control over my circumstances." Determined to have the family she always wanted, Anna didn't give up on her dreams, and she and her husband decided to try IVF.

The decision to pursue IVF was a path that led her into a difficult season of resentment in her marriage, frustration toward God, and emotional and financial depletion. After hundreds of shots and two failed IVF retrievals, they were done. "We were completely spent in every way, and we were left picking up the pieces of, now what?" As Anna began questioning her life, she also began seeing glimpses of God's faithfulness in real time.

It was Easter week when God gave Anna one of those glimpses. As she contemplated the cross and the emotions the disciples must have been feeling, a revelation came to her. "Sometimes God is silent. Sometimes you don't get the answer that you so desperately want, and sometimes heartbreak and hopelessness grab hold of you, and it can seem like it's the end. Sometimes you have to simply sit in the heartbreak of reality, looking so, so different from what you thought it would. But the beauty of the gospel is that the worst thing to happen is not the last thing, because Sunday did come, and He is risen." Anna began to see God's faithfulness in a new light, and this hope gave her the strength she needed to move forward.

God's faithfulness is the solid foundation for all Believers. It is the rock on which we build our lives, knowing He is trustworthy to keep His promises. His faithfulness provides a steady place to stand when the ground beneath us shakes with suffering and sorrow. It gives us height when we need perspective to see above the chaos and confusion. It supplies a stable strength to lean on when despair and disbelief try to take us down. God's unchanging faithfulness is the catalyst that sparks the fire of hope within us.

The meaning of faithfulness in the Bible conveys the idea of a reliable, steadfast trust. So, when Scripture tells us God is faithful, it proclaims His trustworthiness. And God's trustworthiness solidly rests on the belief that He is incapable of breaking His promises. When God says He will do something, you can rest assured He will. When God says His character encompasses something, you can know, with certainty, it does. When God says His authority over your life is unequivocally dependable, you can place all bets on it that it is. God's trustworthy faithfulness allows you to hold onto, without hesitation, the hope you have in Jesus Christ (Heb. 10:23).

Time and time again, throughout the Old Testament, God shows us He is true to His promises. God was faithful from the days of Noah, promising never again to flood the earth (He even gave us the rainbow as a sign of His unbreakable promise). God was faithful to Abraham, giving him land, a nation, and a lasting name. God was faithful in delivering the Israelites from slavery in Egypt. God was faithful to King David when He assured him that a King from his lineage would reign forever. God was faithful to the Jewish people to bring them back to Jerusalem after being exiled in Babylon. We could go on and on recounting stories of God's faithfulness to His children.

God's faithfulness is further seen in the New Testament through the culmination of His greatest promise: the sending of His One and only Son, Jesus Christ. This promise served as the pinnacle of God's rescue mission to bring His children back into an intimate relationship with Him and offer the gift of eternal life to all who would believe (John 3:16). It was a promise thousands of years in the making. It was a promise that showcased God's perfect love and one that required the ultimate sacrifice. And it is a promise that, based on His faithfulness, should ignite a bonfire of trust deep within our souls.

Today, reflect on God's faithfulness. Reflect on Jesus' faithfulness on the cross that reconciled your relationship with God. Sit in remembrance of what He has done for you over the years. How has His faithfulness blessed you or pursued you? How has His faithfulness been your strength or protection? How has He been faithful in moments where you were faithless? Give thanks to God for all He's done in your life and for His faithfulness that endures forever.

As Anna began asking herself questions about her faith, she recognized that it is in the messy middle of life that you need God's truth the most. "There is purpose in the pain, even when we can't find it or understand it. God is using each little story to drive the narrative of His big story." And while Anna recognizes the outcome of her story wasn't what she would have chosen, she rests in the knowledge that God is faithful to take what the enemy meant for evil and turn it to good. "The most valuable of all the lessons that we have learned is that God really is faithful, even when the answer is no. What I want each of you to take away from this story is that the Lord sustains no matter the circumstances. When you're in the messy middle of a storm, sometimes you just want to know that you're not alone, or that you can survive it. I'm here to say that God is indeed faithful. He can take our broken pieces and turn them into a masterpiece."

A Closing Prayer

Lord, your faithfulness overwhelms me. When I think of the ways you have shown your faithfulness to me over the years, I am filled with overflowing gratitude for your kindness and love. I especially want to thank you for being faithful to me when I have been faithless to you. Thank you for being a promise-keeper, trustworthy and true. I praise you for your faithfulness today. Amen.

To listen to Anna's story, go to www.storytellerslive.org/wherehopemeetsyou and look for "God's Unchanging Faithfulness"

Day 31

Hope in the Promise of Eternal Life

"Blessed be the God and Father of our Lord Jesus Christ!
According to his great mercy, he has caused us to be born again
to a living hope through the resurrection of Jesus Christ
from the dead, to an inheritance that is imperishable, undefiled,
and unfading, kept in heaven for you."
—1 Peter 1:3–4

After Toma met the Lord in college, she developed an insatiable hunger to memorize God's Word. It came as a prompting from the man who would become her husband. But looking back, Toma can see it was a precious gift the Lord gave her to prepare her for what was to come in her life.

Over the years, she and her husband continued to pour themselves into Scripture. They worked together in ministry, and the Lord blessed them with six children. However, with those blessings came heartbreak. Two and a half weeks before Toma's second child was born, he passed away prematurely. It was the Word of God, stored deep in her soul, that got her through his passing. She told the Lord, "We don't understand, but we trust you, and we're surrendering our lives completely to you and this baby to you."

Many years later, this surrendered trust steadied her to face yet another tragedy in her life—, the news that her 26-year-old son, Ben, had fallen off the side of a mountain while on a hike and died. "We prayed, and we asked the Lord to be there. He's already shown His faithfulness before, and we knew He was going to do it again because He is the same yesterday, today, and forever."

In the days after Ben's passing, the Lord gave Toma a peace and strength she couldn't explain. She knew it was straight from God. Once again, Scripture flooded her heart. "He told us that in this world we would have much trouble, but with Him we would overcome the world. He also tells us that our light and momentary troubles are achieving for us an eternal glory that far outweighs them all. So, we need to fix our eyes not on what we can see, for that is temporary, but on what we can't see, which is eternal. He's got an eternal purpose in all of our pain. To walk by faith and not by sight, I must learn to live life in the light of eternity with my heart and mind set on Jesus."

If you knew you were going to Heaven next week to meet Jesus, how would your life be different in your last days on earth? Would you overflow with love and forgiveness to those around you? Would you speak more kindly and offer more compassion? Would you face the difficulties in your life with patience and peace? Would it light a fire in your soul to tell others of your faith? How would knowing eternity was a week away change you?

Regardless of when you are going to see Jesus face-to-face, the hope found in His promise of eternal life *should* change you. This hope should propel you to live more like Him every day, allowing (as John the Baptist said) for Jesus to become greater and for you to become less (John 3:30). This hope should open your eyes to live not as a citizen of this world but as a citizen of Heaven (Phil. 3:20). This hope should give you the courage to face each day with confidence as you set your mind on things above (Col. 3:2) and fix your eyes on what is unseen (2 Cor. 4:18). Eternal life is more than a faraway land; it is the guaranteed inheritance you will receive as a daughter of the King (1 Peter 1:3-4). And, what a glorious inheritance it will be!

If the image of the new creation God will usher in, described in Revelation 21, is any indication, the promise of eternal life will be beyond beautiful, brilliantly shining with the glory of God. There will be no more death. No more crying. No more pain. God will be with His children, and nothing impure will ever enter it. Eternity with God will be a place of immense delight and joy (Isaiah 65:18). A place where we will be reunited with those who have gone before us (1 Thess. 4:13-17). A place where we will be made complete in the image of Christ (1 John 3:2). A place where the love of God fills the air and where righteousness dwells (2 Peter 3:13). No wonder we are told no one can imagine the things God is preparing for those who love Him (1 Cor. 2:9). Eternal life will be immeasurably more than we could ask for or imagine. The hope of it should have us rejoicing every day about our future.

As you reflect on your own coming home ceremony, allow yourself to relish in the beauty that awaits you in Paradise (Luke 23:43). Sit in gratefulness knowing Jesus Himself is preparing a room for you (John 14:2). Consider the great cloud of witnesses who are cheering you on as you run this race of life (Heb. 12:1). Imagine what it will be like when you see the Lord face to face (1 Cor. 13:12). This is your ultimate hope. *Eternal Life*. Leverage your life for eternity today, and live knowing it's all for Jesus.

As Toma continued to focus her eyes on eternity, the Lord was kind enough to show her the purpose in Ben's death. While Ben had given his life to Jesus at the age of 12, in his later years, he was their prodigal child. "Why did the Lord take him before he became a mighty man of God? We don't know, but we do know our God does no wrong. And, so we trust in His ways, that He is good. He took him for a reason."

Soon after Ben's passing, Toma discovered one of those possible reasons. The young man who found Ben at the bottom of the mountain was not a Believer either. However, in God's compassionate mercy, the young man told Toma and her husband, "I want you to know that when Ben took his last breath, I felt the presence of the Lord all around us." It was incredibly comforting for Toma to hear, and even more comforting to find out that the young man who found Ben came to know the Lord.

Toma's hope remains steadfast on the promise of eternal life. "Trust is believing that He is who He says He is and will do what He says He will do. One day, He will wipe every tear from our eyes. There will be no more death or mourning or crying or pain. He will make all things new. What a glorious day that will be. Until then, He is our unshakable hope, and because He is with us, we will not be shaken."

A Closing Prayer

Gracious Heavenly Father, you alone are my hope. I desire to live for you with eternity at the forefront of my mind. When I succumb to the things of this world, refocus my eyes on what is unseen and eternal. I desperately want to leave a legacy that glorifies you in my life. Give me the courage to be bold in my faith and to live as if today is the day I will see you face to face. Thank you, Lord, for the promise of eternal life and the hope it gives me to live for you. Amen.

To listen to Toma's story, go to www.storytellerslive.org/wherehopemeetsyou and look for "Hope in the Promise of Eternal Life."

An Invitation

Continue Living with Hope and Feeding Your Faith

As you have seen over the past 31 days, the hope found in Jesus is powerful. It is the fuel to your faith. It is the catalyst to your contentment. It is the reassurance to your soul. And it's something the Lord doesn't want you to live without. The essence of the gospel message is the good news that because of Jesus, you can live with hope every day. This is also the mission of the *StoryTellers Live* ministry.

If you have been encouraged in your faith through this devotional and want to hear more impactful stories of the hope found in Jesus, consider signing up for the *StoryTellers Live* weekly email. Each Wednesday, you are notified by email about a new story being dropped on the podcast. You can sign up at storytellerslive.org, where you can also find out more about the ministry, including where our live gatherings are taking place. If you live nearby, we would love for you to visit one!

Or maybe you would like to dig into Scripture more deeply and continue discovering God through stories of hope, freedom, and faith. If so, think about going through one of the *StoryTellers Live* Bible studies in the "When God Shows Up" series (available on Amazon or ironhillpress.com). They are perfect for small-group or individual study, as you take the theme of a story from the podcast and delve into what God's Word says about it.

Our challenge for you is to remain steadfast in your search for the hope found in Jesus in your own life. Continue to be still in His presence and reflect on all the Lord has done for you over the years. If you aren't a member of a local church, maybe now is the time to step out and consider joining one? After all, God created you for community, and the church body is a wonderful place to help you continue to see and live from the hope God desires for you.

In closing, we pray this devotional has given you inspiration, insight, wisdom, and understanding; that you have experienced Jesus in new and profound ways; that His love for you and faithfulness to you have been seen and felt; and that as you continue to discover His hope in your own life, you will be a witness of the hope found in Jesus to others (1 Peter 3:15).

May God's favor and blessing be upon you.

With Love,
The *StoryTellers Live* Ministry

About The Author

Katie Dunn is one of the hosts of the *StoryTellers Live* podcast, where everyday women share personal stories of the hope found in Jesus. She also serves as the Discipleship and Content Manager for The *StoryTellers Live* Ministry. She is the author of the *When God Shows Up Bible* study series, which invites women to encounter the truths of hope, freedom, and faith woven throughout Scripture, as well as *Finding God in the Details: A Guide to Discerning God's Voice and Discovering Your Story*, a reflection of her heart for helping others recognize God's presence in the ordinary moments of life.

Katie holds a double major in Mass Communications and Journalism from Auburn University and has completed coursework through Beeson Divinity School's Lay Academy. A devoted student of God's Word, she has spent more than two decades crafting and leading Bible studies, walking alongside women as they learn to encounter God personally through Scripture. She is passionate about creating spaces where women feel seen, encouraged, and grounded in the unchanging truth of God's promises.

Katie lives in Birmingham, Alabama, with her husband of thirty-one years, Allen; they have two adult children. When she isn't writing or teaching, she can often be found on a long walk with friends or playing with her labradoodle, Addie.

IRON HILL

press

Equipping the Church
to know God
through His Word.